NEW REVISED EDITION with all the latest treatments now available

regaining potency
the answer to male impotence

OLIVER GILLIE

SELF-HELP DIRECT

◆

Acknowledgements

With many thanks for their interest and help to Mr John Pryor MBBS FRCS, Mr Gordon Williams MBBS FRCS, Dr Elizabeth Stanley MRCS and Dr Ronald Virag

◆

More copies of this book are available from Self-Help Direct Publishing, PO Box 9035, London, N12 8ED. Price: £10.95 cheque or postal order (postage & packing free) (overseas sales $25 per book) payable to *Self-Help Direct*. Bulk order prices on application.

Our promise: If you are not satisfied with any of our books, we will refund your money if you return the book in good condition within 10 days

◆

DESIGN: Michael Crozier/Design Unlimited
COVER ILLUSTRATION: Michael Daley
GRAPHIC page 5: Roy Cooper

◆

Published by Self-Help Direct Publishing, PO Box, London, N12 8ED
First edition 1995. Second edition 1997

ISBN 1 900461 20 X

contents

introduction

About one in ten men have difficulty obtaining a sufficiently strong erection to have full sexual intercourse with their partner. Difficulty in obtaining erections can be caused by anxiety or other psychological factors but in recent years doctors have come to realise that long term difficulty is often caused by a physical problem of some kind – particularly in older men. This discovery has brought new treatments and new hope for many men.

Instead of being told that the problem is in their head and they need to talk more about it with their partner or with a therapist, there is now the possibility of drug treatment, surgery and various devices that can assist in producing an erection. Even so the problem remains a psychological one for a significant proportion of men and for them the possibility of a physical solution is sometimes helpful or at least serves to define the problem. Indeed for many men it is essential to provide a combined approach because body and mind must work together to produce a good erection.

Men with erection problems are often referred to as being impotent – a term which recognises the deep connection between mind and body when it comes to sexual matters. Difficulty in obtaining erections can sap a man's confidence and affect other areas of his life. On the other hand, a man who has never had erection problems may encounter them for the first time when he has a crisis in some other part of his life and becomes anxious or depressed as a result. However the word impotence is loaded with meaning which is not relevant to the experience of many men with erection difficulties and so doctors now tend to prefer the term erectile dysfunction.

The penis contains three spongy chambers which become filled with blood during an erection. As a result the penis becomes hard enabling entry into the vagina. For an erection to occur the nerves and blood vessels supplying the penis must be working adequately and a man must be producing sufficient male hormones. It is recognised that erection may be prevented by physical illness such as diabetes or by blood vessel disease that may also cause angina and heart attacks, as well as by damage to nerves and blood vessels from accidents or surgery.

Healthy men normally have erections during the night while they are sleeping and often on waking in the morning. Men who have physical illness or damage which prevents erections during loveplay are generally unable to have erections during the night. Men whose problem is psychological generally have normal erections at night. These and other ways can be used to indicate whether an erection problem is primarily physical or psychological.

Whatever the cause of the problem women often feel that it is their fault that their partner cannot obtain an erection. They may feel that their partner no longer loves them or is attracted to them and perceive the difficulty with erection as a rejection. Even when a problem is physical a man may not understand and so may blame his wife for being unattractive or consider his failure to respond sexually as evidence that the relationship is burnt out. For these sort of reasons erectile dysfunction can be very destructive of relationships and put couples under an enormous strain.

A million and a half men in Britain, both heterosexual and homosexual, suffer permanently from erection problems and about five million men have suffered from impotence at some time according to a survey by the drug company Upjohn. However, there are now many ways in which men with erection problems can be helped to have a good and fully satisfying sex life. This book looks at the causes of impotence and describes the various different types of help now available and where to get them. There are now a wide variety of treatments available providing help for every type of problem.

How to identify your problem and find your way around this book

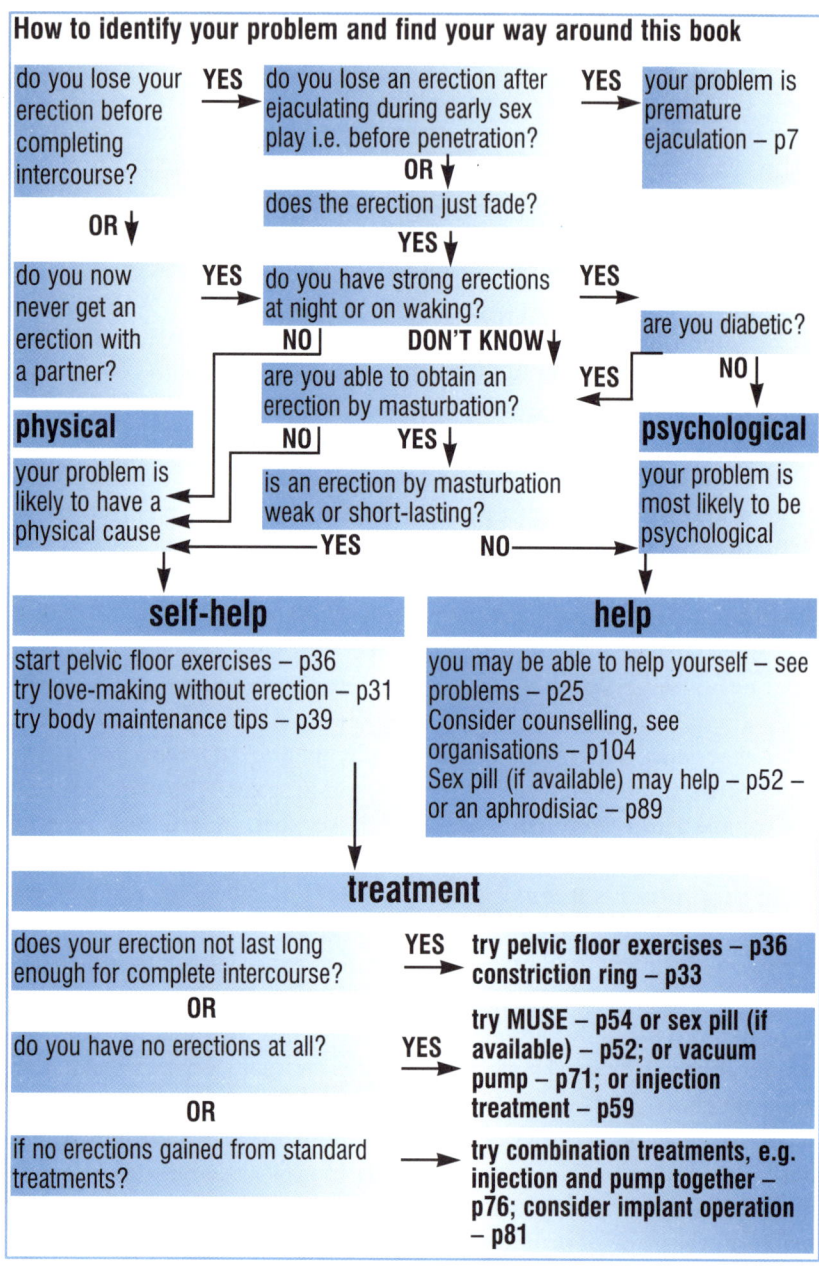

do you lose your erection before completing intercourse?

YES → do you lose an erection after ejaculating during early sex play i.e. before penetration? **YES** → your problem is premature ejaculation – p7

OR ↓

does the erection just fade?

YES ↓

OR ↓

do you now never get an erection with a partner? **YES** → do you have strong erections at night or on waking? **YES** →

NO | **DON'T KNOW** ↓

are you diabetic?

NO ↓

are you able to obtain an erection by masturbation? **YES** ←

physical

your problem is likely to have a physical cause

NO | **YES** ↓

is an erection by masturbation weak or short-lasting?

—— **YES**

psychological

your problem is most likely to be psychological

NO ——→

self-help

start pelvic floor exercises – p36
try love-making without erection – p31
try body maintenance tips – p39

help

you may be able to help yourself – see problems – p25
Consider counselling, see organisations – p104
Sex pill (if available) may help – p52 – or an aphrodisiac – p89

treatment

does your erection not last long enough for complete intercourse?

OR

do you have no erections at all?

OR

if no erections gained from standard treatments?

YES → **try pelvic floor exercises – p36 constriction ring – p33**

YES → **try MUSE – p54 or sex pill (if available) – p52; or vacuum pump – p71; or injection treatment – p59**

→ **try combination treatments, e.g. injection and pump together – p76; consider implant operation – p81**

◆ 4 ◆

regaining potency: the answer to male impotence

specific problems

Do you smoke?	➤ smoking is a major cause of impotence but potency may return if you quit – p39
Do you take prescribed drugs?	➤ many prescribed drugs are associated with impotence – p16 consult your doctor – p15
do you take any non-medicinal drugs for recreational purposes?	➤ many drugs affect libido and mood – you may have to choose between pleasures – p18
is your waist over 40 inches?	➤ overweight is a contributory problem – p45
are you over 45?	➤ fitness is likely to be a problem – work hard on the pelvic floor exercises and the body maintenance – p36, 37, 39
are you a regular drinker?	➤ more than 3 units of alcohol (I unit=1 glass of wine, 1 measure of spirits, 1/2 pint beer) a day can affect erections – p48
has your erection failed in a new relationship?	➤ the cause is probably performance anxiety and is likely to be temporary – p14
are you often angry with your partner?	➤ it is difficult for a man to be aroused if he is angry – p12
does your partner fondle your penis and/or arouse you with oral sex?	➤ if she does not, this may be all you need – p25

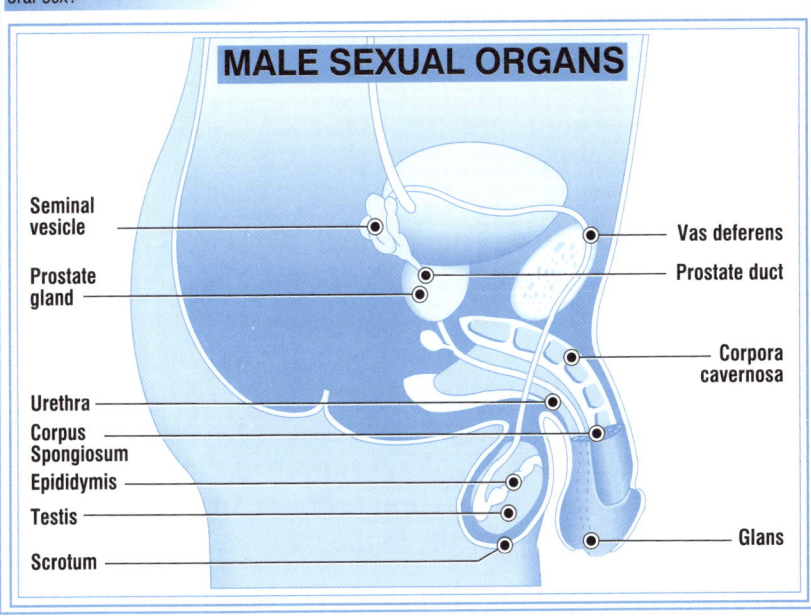

MALE SEXUAL ORGANS

Seminal vesicle — Vas deferens
Prostate gland — Prostate duct
— Corpora cavernosa
Urethra
Corpus Spongiosum
Epididymis
Testis
Scrotum — Glans

CHAPTER ONE:
diagnosis of erectile problems

Is it not strange that desire should so many years outlive performance?
Henry IV, Part Two, II:4
William Shakespeare (1546 - 1616)

physical or psychological

If the penis is not firm enough for entry into the vagina, or does not remain firm sufficiently long for intercourse to be completed, there is clearly an erection problem. The next step is to discover if the problem is caused by physical or psychological factors.

If a man is able to get a hard erection by masturbation, or is having normal hard erections at night or on waking in the morning this generally shows that he does not have a physical problem. However, some men are not aware of their night time erections. Others may have weak night time erections or be uncertain how satisfactory they are.

It is now possible to test the strength of a man's erection by injection of a drug directly into the penis. The penis will then become erect within about ten minutes provided the blood supply is adequate. If a man has a good erection when these drugs are injected but does not have hard erections at night or when attempting to masturbate then he probably has a physical problem with the blood supply to the penis. This is the commonest form of erection problem in older men who have had a satisfactory sex life in the past.

A man who has a psychological problem may find an erection induced by injection to be immensely encouraging and find that he can use it effectively, especially if given psychological support by a therapist. However, a few men find it frightening and after one experience of an injection erection are quite sure that they do not wish to attempt intercourse with an erection induced that way. Of course there is no need for such fear since the injection itself is not painful.

Often it is impossible to separate the physical and psychological aspects of erection. Men who have a clear physical problem that is capable of being treated successfully often require a great deal of psychological support as well. And men whose problem is psychological obtain encouragement when they see clear evidence from injection of drugs that their sex apparatus is in full working order.

premature ejaculation and other problems

Some men who believe they have difficulty with erection are actually ejaculating prematurely. When a man ejaculates before entry of the penis into the vagina or very early in intercourse he generally loses his erection quite rapidly. This type of sexual response, called premature ejaculation, is sometimes confused with difficulty in obtaining an erection. Men who ejaculate prematurely do not generally have any difficulty in obtaining a firm erection on initiation of loveplay.

If an erection is sufficiently hard to enable entry into the vagina then erection itself is not the problem, even if ejaculation occurs shortly after entry. Even when ejaculation occurs before entry can take place, erection is not the problem if the penis has become hard and capable of entry. In these cases the man is ejaculating prematurely. There are now well-established methods for treating premature ejaculation which are available as part of sex therapy. *(Relate – Marriage Guidance, for example, provides counselling for this type of problem, see page 104)*

Many men who ejaculate prematurely find it helpful to use a rubber constriction ring at the base of the penis to maintain their erection. The constriction ring delays the return of the blood to the body maintaining the penis in a rigid state after ejaculation. This enables a man to begin intercourse or continue with it after ejaculation. Using the ring a man may satisfy his partner and take her to orgasm – provided there are no other difficulties. *(For details about constriction rings, see panel, page 74)*

A number of other common problems are confused with impotence. Many women think that a man should be able to get an erection simply by willing it or by thinking about sex. Young men often do get erections very easily with little or no sexual provocation. However as men get older these spontaneous erections become increasingly rare. The sight of a woman in an erotic situation is not sufficient to sexually arouse most older men who have, after all, generally seen something similar many times before both on and off the screen. An older man may need to be made aware that the woman is sexually available, interested – and even keen – before he is aroused. An older man also takes longer to fully recover his sexual capability after an orgasm. A young man may be able to have intercourse twice within an hour but an older man will generally take some hours or even days before recovering the ability to have another erection.

A common problem is insufficient foreplay in the form of playful flirting before attempting intercourse. Some women expect intercourse to occur with little or no direct stimulation of the penis. An older man often needs plenty of direct stimulation to the penis with hand and/or mouth before he will obtain an erection. Women who have not been used to taking an active part in sex may find this difficult and the couple may benefit from counselling. Many couples find that a vibrator (available from sex shops or by mail order) can be helpful. Use the vibrator in a teasing way to stimulate the penis – do not be afraid to experiment. Use the vibrator on your partner as well if she is interested in trying it. A more romantic atmosphere will also help so that both man and woman can relax and enjoy thoughts of love before moving on to any direct action. Candlelight, soft music, pleasant food, are all helpful.

Couples often fall into a habit of thinking that lovemaking should end in intercourse. Or, fearful that lovemaking may lead to failure, avoid the cuddles and playful contact that may eventually lead on easily to penetration and orgasm.

If the idea that intercourse must occur can be avoided then other enjoyable contact may be easier – try for example a massage with special oils. Massage oils can be bought at most chemists. Intercourse may occur sometimes following such playful contact but if it does not there is no need for disappointment. In fact some couples discover that they can happily make love in exciting ways without the man having an erection. *(See Lovemaking without a full erection, page 31)*

Sometimes a man may believe that he is impotent when he has no physical problem, or be told by his partner that he is impotent when in fact the problem is caused by something else. A man may lose his erection, for example, if the woman complains of pain in intercourse or does not participate in lovemaking. A man may also lose his erection if he perceives that the woman is not entirely receptive. A woman may indicate willingness for intercourse but not be well lubricated, or she may express some modification of feeling that the man finds rejecting so causing him to lose his erection. These problems can sometimes be overcome with the help of a water based lubricant and some goodwill, but other couples need to talk more about it together, and some will find counselling helpful. Counselling and sex therapy are available from a number of different organisations. *(See page 104)*

CHAPTER TWO:
causes of erection problems

*If sex is such a natural phenomenon, how come
there are so many books on how to?*
Bette Midler, actress and comedienne

Experts do not agree on what proportion of men with erection problems have a physical cause of their problem and what proportion have a psychological cause. As many as 80 per cent of men going to a doctor with erection problems have a physical cause for their difficulty but many also have psychological complications. About 10 per cent of men have a purely physical problem and about 10 per cent have a purely psychological problem. The opinion of experts is coloured by their experience: doctors tend to recognise more cases of physical erection problems whereas marriage guidance experts see a lot of erection problems related to emotional difficulties. Surveys suggest that in eight out of 10 men with an erection problem the primary cause is physical rather than psychological. However many of these men who began with a physical problem develop psychological problems as well because failure brings lack of confidence.

psychological causes

Men who are suffering from depression, anxiety state, grief and similar psychological conditions are often unable to obtain an erection. A problem with erections may also develop when a relationship enters a difficult emotional phase.

Most men have experienced a temporary difficulty in obtaining an erection as a result of tiredness, alcohol, or an emotional problem. For the majority of such men normal potency returns very soon, although for some a single failure may have a drastic effect on confidence which causes a self-perpetuating problem. When this happens the man and his partner will most easily be helped by psychotherapy which helps them to talk about the problem and guide them back to successful intercourse.

A man may, for example, begin to have difficulty with his potency on being made redundant or on experiencing financial loss. The male sexual response is not nearly so robust as is popularly imagined.

"Anything which makes a man feel badly about himself can erode his sexual responsiveness," says Dr Elizabeth Stanley, senior lecturer in Human Sexuality at St George's Hospital, Tooting. "Failure to deal with anger which arises in a relationship is one of the commonest causes of problems with erections. If emotional problems are not openly expressed in a relationship then it's very difficult to talk through a problem. Hidden resentments may build up – sometimes over years – and cause problems with erections."

Another problem for some men and women is a subconscious feeling that sex is dirty and that nice people don't do it together. Some men may be able to have a satisfactory sexual relationship in a short-term affair, or with a prostitute, but not with their wife.

"Sex therapy can help a couple recognise these sorts of problems," says Dr Stanley. "A man may sometimes become impotent because he loses confidence in his sexual ability. He may have failed to have an erection once because he was tired and then be afraid it will happen again. One such failure early on in the honeymoon may lead to years of impotence. Good sex is all to do with good communication – being able to tell your partner what you like and don't like. It means getting rid of this dreadful myth that men know exactly what to do to arouse a woman. And that it's not for the woman to give her partner any information. Sex therapy helps a couple talk about their problems."

Zilbergeld's myths

Many men have unrealistic attitudes and beliefs about sex. Bernard Zilbergeld, a distinguished sexologist working at the University of California, has written out a list of these beliefs which have become known as Zilbergeld's myths. *(See panel)*

These myths act as a psychological straitjacket for many men. Without stopping to try to analyse a situation or watch for cues from their partner they believe that everything depends on them. They also believe that sex should be natural and spontaneous but at the same

the myths

1. In general a man should not be seen to express certain emotions
2. In sex, as elsewhere, it is performance that counts
3. An erection is essential for a satisfying sexual experience
4. All physical contact must lead to sex
5. Sex equals intercourse
6. Good sex must follow a linear progression of increasing excitement and terminate in orgasm
7. Sex should be natural and spontaneous
8. On the whole the male must take charge of and orchestrate sex
9. A man always wants and is ready for sex

time try to take charge – the result is a series of conflicts often culminating in what has been called performance anxiety.

Anxiety often builds up as the man worries whether he is going to be able to achieve an erection and whether he will be able to maintain it. The more he becomes preoccupied with this anxiety the more he is distracted from foreplay and so the sexual stimulus is reduced and the erection lost. These problems can occur whatever a man's sexual orientation, whether gay or straight.

Men who are having difficulty obtaining or maintaining an erection often end all sexual activity in their lives. They do not want to put themselves in a position where their difficulty may be revealed. The man and his partner then drift further apart than they need because kissing, fondling and, even simple touching, cease. The woman often perceives this as the man no longer loving her and she feels rejected. Anger and hostility builds up and the couple begin to find it very difficult to live with each other.

The drift apart can often be prevented by sexual activity without intercourse which can be just as satisfying for many women – indeed many women find it more satisfying than intercourse itself. *(See lovemaking without a full erection, page 31)*

physical causes

Difficulty in obtaining erections can be caused by a number of different diseases, by accidental injury, as a result of an operation, or by drugs prescribed by your doctor. It is advisable to consult your doctor if you have had a persistent problem in obtaining erections because it may be the first sign of diabetes, high blood pressure, or heart disease. Early warning of the development of these conditions should be counted as a blessing since much can be done to overcome the problems by alteration of lifestyle *(see page 39)* and, when necessary, drug treatment.

Drugs prescribed for high blood pressure, depression and certain other conditions may cause inadequate erections or contribute to the problem. Some drugs reduce erections because they affect mood or libido, others have a more direct effect by altering blood supply or response of tissues. If you are taking drugs and have erection problems then it is important to discuss the matter with your doctor. Often it is possible to change the drugs being taken or to reduce the dose so that adequate erections may be obtained. For example, diuretics ("water tablets" used to prevent fluid retention) and beta blockers taken for high blood pressure may interfere with erection and may often be changed to vasodilator drugs which do not have this effect. *(A list of drugs which are known to interfere with erections in some men is given in the panel on page 16)*

Diabetes is one of the commonest diseases to cause difficulty in obtaining erections. However, because of the embarrassment, which has generally prevented discussion of erection problems, the British Diabetic Association has only recently recognised erectile dysfunction as a complication of the disease. In the past there was no mention of erection difficulty in their literature and the majority of diabetic men

drugs which may cause erection failure

Drugs in the table are listed under broad categories and then a few examples are given using the scientific name of the drug. Drugs may be prescribed by a doctor using either the scientific name or the brand name. It is not possible to give a complete list of drugs which affect erections and so any man who has erection difficulties and is also taking medication should discuss the problem with his doctor. Whether or not a particular drug interferes with erections will depend on the dose of the drug and on the health of a man's blood vessels and nerves. Often it is possible to either reduce the dosage of a drug or to change to another drug which does not affect erections.

major tranquillisers
phenothiazines: for example: fluphenazine, chlorpromazine, promazine, mesoridazine
butyrophenones: for example: haloperidol
thiozanthines: for example: thiohixene, chlorprothixine

antidepressants
tricyclics: for example: nortryptyline, amitriptyline, desipramine, doxepin
MAO inhibitors: for example: isocarboxazide, phenelzine, tranylcypromine, pargylene, procarbazine

tranquillisers
benzodiazepines: for example: chlordiazepoxide, diazepam, chorazepate

anticholinergics
atropine, propantheline, benztrophine, dimenhydrinate,diphenhydramine

antihypertensives
diuretics: for example: thiazides, spironolactone
vasodilators: for example: hydralazine
central sympatholytics: for example: methyldopa, clonidine, reserpine
ganglion blockers: for example: guanethidine, bethanidine
alpha-blockers: for example: phenoxybenzamine, prazosin
beta-blockers: for example: propranolol, metoprolol, atenolol

miscellaneous
cimetidine, clofibrate, cyproterone acetate, digoxin, oestrogens, indomethacin

were treated as if their erection problems had a psychological cause. This has now changed and the British Diabetic Association will supply diabetics with helpful information and with some counselling. *(See page 105)*

Diabetes damages nerves and blood vessels throughout the body and so reduces the circulation of blood in the penis as well as in other extremities such as the feet and hands. The condition generally becomes progressively worse in diabetics until all ability to obtain a spontaneous erection is lost. However, diabetics often go on getting erections during sleep and in the morning and this has sometimes misled doctors into thinking that the cause of their problem is psychological. Drugs, injections, vacuum pump therapy or, in the most difficult cases, insertion of an implant into the penis are all possible ways of helping men with diabetes.

It is well-known that too much alcohol may make a man incapable of having sex. It is less well-known, however, that regular consumption of substantial quantities of alcohol may permanently reduce a man's sexual desire. This happens because alcohol causes a loss of masculine body features. Damage to the liver from alcohol reduces the production of male hormone in the liver and heavy drinkers who are overweight may also have an increased production of female hormone. Reduction in alcohol consumption can reverse this effect and enable a man to obtain good erections once more.

Raised blood pressure is also associated with an increased risk of erection problems. The hardening of the arteries that is associated with high blood pressure occurs progressively with age, causing angina and making men and women vulnerable to heart attacks. Some people suffer from severe "anginal" pain in the legs when walking. The localised pain in the legs is caused by failure of damaged arteries to provide enough oxygen to the muscles. As people age, arteries throughout the body often become narrowed, and in some cases blocked, by deposits of atheroma, a fatty material, in the vessel walls. These deposits cut down the blood circulation, reducing the supply of oxygen to the tissues, and in the extreme situation, angina or a heart attack is the result.

The same deposits of atheroma occur in arteries of the pelvis which supply the penis with blood. So men who have large deposits of atheroma in their arteries may have difficulty obtaining an erection even when they feel fully aroused sexually and are eager to have intercourse. The deposits blocking the arteries will not allow a fast enough flow of blood into the penis to allow erection. This difficulty can now be overcome in a number of ways – by drugs or with a vacuum pump which are described later in the book.

Heavy smoking is an important cause of furring up of arteries and giving up smoking will prevent further deterioration. But there are also short term benefits from giving up smoking. Tobacco smoke causes the constriction of veins and carbon monoxide in tobacco smoke reduces the capability of the blood for carrying oxygen. So giving up smoking will provide immediate benefits by an increase in blood supply and oxygen to tissues. Recreational drugs such as marijuana, cocaine and heroin may also interfere with erections either by alteration of mood or less directly by alteration of the amount of the male hormone, testosterone, circulating in the body.

A Northern European diet which contains a lot of animal fat and relatively little fruit and vegetables is thought by many doctors to be another cause of disease of the arteries, often causing erection problems in men from the late 40s and 50s on. An increase in blood fats (hyperlipidaemia) is a well-known risk factor associated with erection problems. This disease of the arteries is less common in Mediterranean countries where oil is generally used in cooking and more vegetables are eaten. Eating the right food will slow down the progression of artery damage giving a longer life and a longer and better love life. *(See the food of love – page 43)*

All the physical causes of erection problems – diet, smoking, and drinking – have greater effect with age and so by the age of 70 six out of 10 men are unable to have erections. A judicious choice of diet, very moderate drinking and no smoking will do much to ensure that a man's sex life is able to continue into his 70s and even longer.

Cycling long distances on a hard narrow saddle may occasionally damage the artery that takes blood to the penis. A saddle should be chosen for comfort, and care should be taken to shift your position on the saddle regularly during a long ride.

Failure to obtain erections may sometimes be caused by surgical operations in the pelvic area which damage nerves and blood vessels going to the penis. Surgery on the prostate, bladder, bowel or rectum may all on occasion result in impotence. Accidents which injure the pelvis and spinal cord are another cause of impotence. However, even in these difficult circumstances erections may be obtained with the help of drugs or a pump, and men may also, with help, be able to ejaculate and so father their own children. Medical help in these circumstances has often done a great deal to help keep couples together in the most testing times.

Multiple sclerosis, a disease of the central nervous system which causes increasing loss of use of the limbs, may also interfere with the nervous responses necessary for an erection. Men who are on dialysis for kidney disease often experience impotence because of nerve or blood vessel damage associated with kidney failure. Men with any of these conditions who also have difficulty in obtaining erections should discuss the problem with their GP or specialist in the first instance. Tests will be necessary to diagnose the cause of the problem fully and find out which type of help is most appropriate. Even if the nerve supply has been badly damaged it may still be possible to obtain an erection and have intercourse using the vacuum pump method or with the help of a surgical implant.

Inability to obtain erections is sometimes the result of low thyroid activity and a few other uncommon conditions. However it rarely occurs as the first sign of these illnesses. Usually erection problems develop later, after these conditions have already been diagnosed. Nevertheless it is a good idea to consult your general practitioner about erection problems and if he thinks the problem is connected with other illness he will be able to enlist the help of a specialist.

CHAPTER THREE:
psychotherapy

The mind can also be an erogenous zone
Colombo's Hollywood (J.R. Colombo)
Raquel Welch, American film star

Psychotherapy used to be the only treatment readily available for erection problems. In the past psychotherapy was given to many men who did not have psychological problems and sometimes caused substantial harm. Many men were led to believe they had a mental block preventing them from having an erection and sexual intercourse when their problem was in fact a physical one resulting from changes in blood vessels and nerves.

A man who is given a psychological interpretation of his problem when in fact it is physical is likely to become confused and angry. Following the diagnosis his partner is likely to interpret his physical inability to have an erection as rejection of her and the results can be extremely damaging. There is a grave danger that a relationship will come apart if an incorrect diagnosis is made which labels the problem as psychological when it is physical. The woman is likely to conclude that her partner does not love her any more or at least not enough to want to have intercourse.

Nevertheless, inability to have an erection often does have a psychological cause. Temporary impotence may occur as a result of anxiety, depression, or stress, and disappear spontaneously once conditions change. Bereavement, worries at work and particularly loss of a job are often the cause of temporary erection problems. Such crises may make a man feel powerless and unable to initiate sex or respond sexually. Sometimes depression, which always reduces libido, is the basic condition inhibiting sexuality. Sometimes a feeling of inadequacy builds up together with a fear of rejection which inhibits the sexual response.

Bereavement may also cause depression or a preoccupation with feelings about the dead person which excludes sexual feelings. Psychotherapy or counselling can often be effective in bringing fears and anxieties under control or in relieving depression, allowing a normal sexual life to be resumed *(see section at the end of the book on how to find a therapist)*. Anti-depressant drugs which can be obtained from a general practitioner may also be helpful if the depression has persisted for a long time and shows no signs of lifting.

However, it can sometimes be difficult to know whether the depression is caused by the erection problem or vice versa. Certainly in some men suffering from both conditions the depression lifts when their erection difficulty is overcome by injection therapy or other means.

Sometimes erectile problems which began because of other worries become established as a regular pattern. This happens when a man becomes anxious about his performance. Failure to obtain an erection on one occasion when a man is tired or preoccupied with worries of some kind may make him anxious the next time that love-making begins.

This performance anxiety can become so acute that it

completely prevents a man from having a serviceable erection. This sort of problem requires specialist counselling or psychotherapy for the couple. The therapist will generally see the man alone initially and at a later stage bring in the partner so they can talk about ways of overcoming the problem together.

Psychotherapy is most likely to be successful, according to the distinguished sexologist Joseph LoPiccolo of the University of Missouri-Columbia, in certain definite circumstances which can be identified by a therapist. They may also be recognised by men or their partners and so they are listed here *(see page 25)*. Recognition of the problem is a big step but it is only the first stage. However, recognising your problem is not always easy and many couples will need help from a psychotherapist to do this. (*See addresses and information at the end of the book*)

If you find you can obtain a hard erection when you masturbate, you need to consider whether you are failing to make the sort of arrangements that provide time for sex, or if there is some problem with your relationship. You may need to think more of your own pleasure. Perhaps your partner is sometimes too demanding and you should think more of what you want to do and when you want to do it. But keep the arrangements low key. Avoid booking that weekend in Paris or the honeymoon suite in Las Vegas. It is wise not to put yourself under pressure to perform. Make time for love-making. Avoid endless evenings out which leave you tired when you get back together. Try to find time at the weekend for intimate moments during the day.

The problems of performance anxiety can often be overcome with a little insight and patience. If you have failed to obtain an erection at a crucial time do not think that you should put yourself to the test again straightaway. Take your time and let it happen naturally. Do not make intercourse the only objective. Take the seduction phase of loveplay slowly and pretend you are only experimenting. Then you will not feel disappointed if you do not achieve penetration. After repeated experiments you may find that you feel less anxious and can sustain your erection longer until eventually you are able to have full intercourse.

If your partner is interested, experimentation with new ways of love-making may be helpful. Talking to your partner about new positions may in itself arouse a despondent penis. You may ask her if she would like to make love standing up or in a rear entry position. If your erection comes and then goes do not panic. If you relax and fondle each other some more it should come back again. And do not rush to insert the penis. Rushing will interfere with your relaxation and may make you lose it. You could ask your partner to insert your penis as she fondles it making the movement a natural part of her love-making.

Some therapists suggest that once you have achieved an erection with your partner you should not make love right away but allow the erection to disappear and then bring it back with more fondling. In this way you will see that an erection never need be "lost" because it will return with the right encouragement.

identifying common problems

1 **Many women do not fondle their partner's penis and do not attempt to stimulate it by oral sex.**
If a man has some physical difficulty in obtaining an erection or is aged over 50 direct stimulation of the penis by the female partner is very helpful in providing a good erection. If the female partner is not providing such stimulation and is hesitant in doing so, then provision of simple directions by a therapist has a good chance of being successful in alleviating the problem.

2 **The female partner is entirely dependent upon the male obtaining an erection and on intercourse for an orgasm.**
A therapist can often provide useful help to a couple when either or both partners do not think that it is normal for the female to obtain an orgasm by manual or oral stimulation and have never considered using a vibrator. Often a couple can be reassured that the female can obtain full sexual satisfaction by alternative methods of stimulation and be instructed in how to use them. The pressure on the man to perform is then greatly relieved.

3 **Failure to understand that ability to get an erection declines with age.**
Men over 50 commonly have more difficulty in obtaining erections and require more direct physical stimulation of the penis to obtain an erection. They also have a longer period after orgasm when they are unable to have another erection. Some couples react with anxiety to these changes creating anxiety between them and so making the situation worse and making erection very difficult to achieve. This difficulty can be overcome with simple explanations from a therapist and instruction in techniques for dealing with the problem.

4 **Unrealistic expectations derived from mistaken beliefs about sexuality.**
Some women have a totally distorted idea of male sexuality and make unrealistic demands for macho performance (*see panel: Zilbergeld's myths*). Sometimes a man has equally distorted ideas of what is being expected of him. A therapist can help a couple develop more realistic expectations of each other.

5 **Anger, resentment and hostility**. When these negative emotions prevail in a relationship much of the time it can be very difficult for a man to be aroused by physical stimulation. This failure can increase anger and hostility making a circle which is very difficult to break. Psychotherapy can sometimes help to reduce such difficulties.

6 **Denial of sex as part of a power play.** Sometimes a man may feel at a disadvantage in the relationship and try to take control by denying sex or rationing it. In this and other ways inability to have an erection may become established as part of a relationship. Such difficulties can sometimes be resolved in therapy when a couple is prepared to take the time necessary to talk about them and try to change their approach to each other.

Once you have entered the vagina continue to be relaxed. Do not immediately begin to make rapid movements, but gently caress your partner and enjoy the closeness. Begin to move your hips and vary the pace. Once the man has maintained a rigid erection and penetrated, most couples will need no more advice. But if you have other problems, and they are common in couples who have been struggling with erection difficulty, – talk it through together. If talking is difficult or not sufficient get professional help from a counsellor. *(See page 104)*

Gay men will be able to obtain some help from their own counselling services such as Gay Switchboard which will refer men on to specialist groups such as Married Gays and the Gay Bereavement Project. (*See information on page 105*)

Drug treatments are already being used successfully for treatment of some men whose difficulty in obtaining an erection is basically psychological. In future, drugs such as Viagra, sometimes called the Sex Pill because it is available in tablet or pill form, are increasingly likely to be used for psychological and physical problems. When anxiety is the basic psychological problem then drugs may be expected to be helpful. But they are not so likely to be helpful when one of the partners is angry with the other, for example. Only certain types of psychological problem can be expected to respond to this type of kick-start. In some cases use of such drugs will only magnify problems. Careful counselling is advisable before trying such drugs if a psychological basis for the problem is suspected.

An aphrodisiac may also be helpful when the problem is one of anxiety. Careful experimentation with aphrodisiacs may be helpful especially if you can involve your partner *(see aAphrodisiacs, page 89)*

CHAPTER FOUR:
physical methods of treatment

Making love is a sovereign remedy for anguish
Birth without violence
Frédérick Leboyer (1918 -) French obstetrician

For the majority of men who have difficulty in obtaining erections the problem is fundamentally physical. Especially if a man has seldom had difficulty in obtaining an erection in the past then the problem is most likely to have a physical basis. However, the longer a physical problem continues without help the more likely a man is to develop complicated feelings about the situation which may not be helpful – and may require help from a counsellor before they can be resolved.

The first step is to get a check up from a general practitioner because the emergence of impotence may be a sign of illness such as diabetes. It is essential to have the necessary tests done to see if there is any problem that needs medical attention. If you are taking prescription drugs then it is wise to ask your doctor if the drugs may be the cause of erection problems and whether another more suitable drug might be prescribed or whether the dose of the drug could be altered. (*See list of drugs which may affect erections, page 16*)

Some general practitioners are unfamiliar with the various treatments that are now available for erection problems. Some are unsympathetic and some simply find it difficult to discuss such an intimate problem. As a result GPs cannot always be relied upon to provide helpful advice. Nevertheless many GPs are keen to help and may know of National Health clinics which can provide advice. New drugs are becoming available *(see page 50)* which will be prescribed by GPs, and so your GP is the logical first port of call. In a few places devices to assist erection or operations can be obtained through the Health Service and referral by a GP is the best way to obtain such help – but often such treatment can only be obtained privately.

There are a number of other organisations which can provide counselling *(see page 104-105)* and discuss options with you. The options are also given clearly in this book. Some of these options, such as the new drugs, injection treatment, or surgical operations, require expert medical help. This help may be obtained from a GP with referral to a hospital urologist or an expert in sexual medicine when necessary. Many private clinics, which are listed in the yellow pages, also offer these treatments but prices vary. It pays to telephone several clinics and compare prices and treatments offered before making an appointment.

There are some clinics which canvas by post and offer free consultations and then demand around £1,000 before treatment commences. It is wise to avoid this type of clinic and shop around for medical help at a more affordable price. Any doctor or clinic who offers a cure, as opposed to treatment, should be considered with the greatest suspicion.

Before trying methods of inducing erection which involve drugs or injections some men may prefer to consider and perhaps try other solutions that involve life style alterations.

The additional advantage of making lifestyle changes is the general improvement in health that will result because erection difficulty is often the first sign of other problems. Some men do not like to take drugs and find it easier and more natural to make lifestyle changes. However many find drugs or injections simpler and quicker than lifestyle changes. All these different approaches are described in the pages that follow. However difficult the problem there is now a solution for almost every man with erection problems if he is sufficiently determined to continue trying.

The simplest non-invasive treatment for impotence and one of the least well-known is pelvic floor exercise. These exercises can easily be done at home and for some men nothing else is necessary. However, pelvic floor exercises have a greater chance of success if combined with a general programme designed to improve health and fitness. Such a programme involves gentle exercise, a few key changes to diet, and cessation or at least moderation of smoking and drinking. Indeed these general health measures are likely to increase the success of any of the treatments. Other possibilities are: new ways of love-making without a full erection and the pump method which induces erection by drawing blood into the penis by negative pressure and holding it there with an elastic ring at the base.

CHAPTER FIVE:
improving potency at home

Extraordinary how potent cheap music is
Private Lives
Noël Coward (1899 - 1973)

So much medical help is now available for erection problems that I would urge any man who thinks he has a problem to seek medical advice without delay. However there are a number of helpful measures which may be taken right away. For some men these simple measures will overcome any difficulties. These measures will also assist men who obtain medical help and go ahead with drug treatments. Drug treatments are more effective if the body and mind are prepared.

love-making without a full erection

If your partner is interested then new methods of love-making may begin right away while you try to increase the strength of erections by pelvic floor exercises and other means of increasing health and fitness outlined in the following pages. It is essential to have frank discussions with your partner about what you want to achieve. Some women are eager to help and to resume love-making while others say they find various methods of assisting erection to be artificial. Some women are not eager to return to regular sexual activity. If this is the case, then counselling may help *(see list of organisations that can help, page 104)* and is advisable before deciding how to proceed.

Being relaxed and without any pressure is important for both partners if they are to experience the best possible sexual response. So it helps if you can create a situation where it does not matter how far you go in your love-making. Begin with cuddling, kissing, fondling each other and chatting in a relaxed way. Remember that a warm bath, a drink, candlelight and your favourite music may all help. Do not start off thinking that full intercourse must be the aim – see how much pleasure you and your partner can obtain from loveplay in an unstressed situation.

A more elaborate preparation to love-making may produce a partial erection, or, even if it does not, may lead to a connection of penis and vagina that is satisfying even when intercourse is not complete. Direct stimulation of the penis with the hand by either partner may induce a partial erection. Stroking the inner thighs and gently pulling the scrotum or pubic hair may help.

It is too much to expect that you will get back quickly to full sex if you have not had intercourse for months or years. When the penis has not been fully stretched for some time it cannot immediately regain its former size or rigidity. So it may benefit from being regularly "exercised" in loveplay that is undemanding.

It is possible to begin intercourse with a soft penis if either partner puts the penis into the vagina – a manoeuvre called stuffing – and the woman uses the vaginal muscles to hold it there. This may actually help you to gain a stronger erection and enable full intercourse. It sometimes helps if the woman sits on top of the man and rotates her pelvis. This slightly twists the penis, stimulating it and at the same time partially trapping the blood inside the penis.

Sex shops which advertise in top-shelf magazines provide a wide range of vibrators, dildos and strap-on penis stiffeners and penis enlargers which may be of interest to some couples. They may enable a couple to engage in more inventive loveplay and help a man and his partner to obtain orgasm more easily. However some of the devices advertised, such as the Blakoe energiser ring and the biopotenzor which claim to provide electric potentiation of the genitals, should not be taken seriously. They are expensive and cannot be recommended.

when an erection is lost too quickly

Various rubber rings can be obtained from medical suppliers (*see panel, page 74*) and sex shops to assist with erection. These are placed at the base of the penis where they tighten to trap the blood inside. They may be used very effectively with a partial erection prolonging the time of erection sufficiently for full intercourse and orgasm. However, they have dangers. If they are put on too tightly they may prevent blood flow in the penis causing a lack of oxygen. This may cause damage and if a man falls asleep with the ring in position, as he might easily do, there is a danger of serious damage.

In practice it is possible to leave a ring that is not uncomfortably tight in position for at least half an hour without danger. Some people have even experimented with elastic bands or with a condom which is cut off and rolled back to the base of the penis. Such improvised methods are not recommended. A specially-fitted ring will be much more comfortable, more effective and safer. Rings may be fitted by measuring the size of the base of the penis in its flaccid (non-erect) state. The safest option for those who can afford it is probably the Erecaid ring which is sculptured to allow some blood flow to continue while it remains in position. In practice it has not been found to be a hazard if a man falls asleep with the Erecaid ring in position. (*See page 74 for details of rings and suppliers*)

exercises for potency

Erection may fail to occur in the normal way because blood leaks too readily from the penis. A number of surgical operations have been devised to reduce blood flow out of the penis by tying off veins around the base. However, blood flow through the veins around the penis is also influenced by the muscular tension of the area, as is blood flow all over the body. This consideration led some surgeons at the Catholic University, Leuven, Belgium, to compare the benefits of surgery with pelvic floor exercises designed to increase muscular tone and restore more normal blood flow at the base of the penis.

The Belgian doctors chose patients at random offering them either an operation or training with pelvic floor exercises. The exercises proved to be as effective as an operation. Four out of 10 patients improved and were able to obtain full sexual function with erections that were adequate for penetration whichever treatment they were given. A further two out of 10 patients from each group observed an improvement in the duration or rigidity of their erection although it was still not sufficient to restore sexual performance.

The doctors concluded: "Surgery was not superior to the pelvic floor training programme either subjectively or objectively. Moreover, a significant improvement was found following the training programme; 42% were satisfied with the outcome and refused surgery. Pelvic floor exercise is a realistic alternative to surgery in patients with mild degrees of venous leakage." (*Pelvic floor exercise versus surgery in the treatment of impotence. H. Claes and L. Baert. British Journal of Urology 1993, vol. 71, pp52-57*)

Some British doctors are sceptical about the benefits of pelvic floor exercises and believe that the good results obtained in the Belgian trial are the result of the patients' enthusiasm. The fact that exercises appear to be as effective as the operation may be explained because the operation itself is not very effective. This operation is seldom done now in Britain. However many Belgian patients did improve as a result of the exercises alone. Physiotherapists who teach these exercises have seen good results and the approach is entirely rational. So they are worth trying.

The exercise regime used by the Belgian doctors aimed to strengthen two muscles called the ischiocavernosus and the bulbocavernosus. They were working on a theory that these two muscles are active during sexual intercourse when they contract and increase the pressure of the blood in the penis. The men were given general muscle consciousness training by physiotherapists and also learnt to distinguish between contractions of the ischiocavernosus muscle and others of the pelvic floor. They were given a home exercise programme to perform in the lying, sitting and standing positions.

A suitable exercise programme is given in the panel below. It is the same set of exercises used by women after childbirth to tighten up the muscles of the pelvic floor. By doing the exercises problems of incontinence and other complications of childbirth may be reduced. Exercise of these muscles has long been thought to improve sexual relations for women by

pelvic floor exercises

The pelvic floor consists of several layers of muscle in the base of the pelvis. These muscles support the bladder and the bowel. Men have two openings in the pelvic floor, the anus and the urethra (urinary tube). In women the vagina also forms an opening in the pelvic floor and it is vital for women to maintain the strength of these muscles because during pregnancy they help support the baby. The importance of these muscles for sexual potency in the male has only been recognised recently.

Exercises

Most of the time men and women use the muscles of the pelvic floor without consciously thinking about it. The pelvic floor muscles are tightened to control the bladder or the bowel and generally we are only aware of them when the bladder or bowel are full.

1 Identify the pelvic floor muscles. To test the effectiveness of your pelvic floor muscles it is helpful to experiment with them while urinating: When you go to the toilet start to urinate – then stop in midflow, drawing up your pelvic floor muscles. Count to four then start urinating again and finish emptying your bladder. After the bladder is completely empty tighten up the pelvic floor muscles again and count to four once more. Another way of locating pelvic floor muscles is to cough – this causes the pelvic floor to move outwards. When you move your bowels you will naturally want to contract the muscles of the anus and pelvic floor when you have finished. Most people do not have much trouble locating these muscles and contracting them.

2 Practice using pelvic floor muscles. Having identified the muscles of the pelvic floor you can then practise using them. By regularly tightening helping to tone up genital muscles which are better able to grip the penis so increasing its stimulation during intercourse.

Difficulty in obtaining erections may also be caused by a slow inflow of blood into the penis caused by partially-blocked arteries, or by damage to nerves in and around the penis. Pelvic floor exercises may help by reducing the speed of outflow of blood so giving more time for it to accumulate in the penis. Since these exercises can only be beneficial and drug treatments are more intrusive it makes sense to try the

them you will build up their strength. The exercises can be done at any time in the sitting or standing position. The basic exercise is to contract the muscles, hold for four seconds and relax. With short rests repeat the cycle at least three or four times – doing the whole exercise at least twice a day. You may find that you hold your breath when you first try the exercise – if you did, then practice doing it again without holding your breath.

3 Advanced exercise of the pelvic floor. After repeating the basic exercise for five days try this more advanced exercise: contract the muscles of the pelvic floor and hold for four seconds as before, then try to contract the muscles a little more passing on to a second stage of tightness. Hold this for four seconds and then see if you can tighten once more to the third stage, and hold again for four seconds.

Relax completely and rest before repeating the cycle. If the muscle of the pelvic floor begins to tremble, release it and rest before trying the exercise again. Try to keep the muscles of your backside, thighs and abdomen relaxed while you tighten the pelvic floor.

These exercises will continue to build up your strength and potency over time – so do not expect instant results. To begin with the muscles will be tired from the exercise itself but after a few days, and certainly after a few weeks, you may expect to see the benefits. Benefit may continue to increase over several months if the exercises are continued. Exercise of these muscles is sufficient to cure impotence in a significant proportion of men. A combination of these exercises with additional attention to diet and lifestyle should be even more effective in helping the return of full natural erections. The exercises may also be effective when used together with a vacuum pump or injections.

exercises first. The exercises are also likely to be helpful if used in conjunction with other treatments and will increase the overall chances of success.

CHAPTER SIX:
body maintenance

The wise, for cure, on exercise depend
To John Driden of Chesterton
John Dryden (1631 - 1700)

After the age of 40 many men begin to suffer from the effects of smoking, lack of exercise and overweight. A traditional British diet plentiful in cakes, biscuits, cheese and other fatty food also begins to take its toll in middle age – the arteries begin to clog up with atheroma and the circulation of the blood to the penis may be reduced.

A modest increase in fitness, a loss in weight, improvement in diet, together with giving up smoking, and reducing drinking can tip the balance of body functions back towards health – and towards better erections. Great benefits are generally felt by men, particularly in the older age groups, when they take these measures to improve their body maintenance. They generally obtain a new sense of well-being and may find that sexual difficulties disappear.

Men who suffer from diabetes or blood vessel disease (peripheral vascular disease) can benefit a great deal from changes in diet which will also improve their general health and delay progress of the disease.

smoking

Giving up smoking is probably the single most important step that you can take to improve health and a vital step if you have erection problems. Smoking has a very bad effect on blood vessels, quite apart from the effect it has on the lungs causing cancer and serious breathing problems. Smoking causes a build-up of atheroma in the arteries, narrowing them and delaying the passage of blood. Narrowing of arteries around the penis is a major cause of difficulty in obtaining erections.

The coronary blood vessels which supply blood to the heart muscle also become narrow as atheroma builds up. One of the coronary vessels may eventually become blocked, cutting off the blood and oxygen supply to an area of the heart muscle causing a heart attack. Arteries in the legs may also be affected causing pain in the legs when walking any distance. So difficulty in obtaining erections is only one reason to give up smoking – the serious effects on arteries and lungs with the prospect of an early death are even more compelling reasons.

When all the effects of smoking are properly understood then many people do not find it so difficult to decide to give up smoking. But giving up smoking can be very difficult because it becomes so much part of a person's life. Smoking is something people often do together, offering cigarettes and accepting them is an important part of life together. If you decide to give up smoking tell your family and friends and ask them to support you and not make it difficult – this is very important.

People often put on weight when they give up smoking. So watch your consumption of snacks. Ordinary chewing gum is a helpful alternative to snacks and contains virtually zero calories. However putting on weight is much less of a hazard to health than smoking so console yourself with the knowledge that you are making the best choice.

exercise

Regular exercise helps to improve the circulation and reduces the risk of heart attack. It lowers blood pressure, reduces blood fat levels and helps to keep weight in check. Regular exercise may also reduce insulin needs in diabetes and help to stabilise the condition. It is important not to begin with a sudden exercise programme. Exercise needs to be graduated according to the fitness of each person. Anyone who is already doing 20 to 30 minutes' exercise three or more times a week is reasonably fit.

Fitness can be most easily increased by walking. For someone not used to walking far, five or ten minutes a day will be all they can manage at first. Do not be discouraged and remember that even a small increase will improve your fitness in the long run and benefit your metabolism. Try to increase your five minute walks gradually and you should feel the benefit. Others will be able to manage 20 minutes, five times a week, which will certainly make an important contribution to fitness. After a week or more, when the walk can be done without feeling unduly tired then it should be increased gradually. At the same time the walking pace should be increased. Ultimately a person who is in good basic health should aim to walk briskly enough to get slightly breathless during the exercise.

So far as possible exercise should be included as part of daily living. For example, you can choose a route to work or shops which involves a walk, you can walk up stairs rather than taking a lift, or you can take up a new activity which involves walking or other exercise. Some people like to take up one activity such as swimming or tennis and get all their exercise that way. A combination of activities is also a good way of keeping fit. For example, swimming once a week, a half hour walk once a week and attending a dance class for an hour could be a good way of getting exercise with variety.

Exercise is in itself invigorating. Natural opiate-like substances are released into the blood stream during exercise causing a mild euphoria. Exercise will help you to sleep and to relax and after a few weeks you will probably notice that you feel much better. The exercise will also help to tone up the muscles of the pelvic floor giving direct help with erections. But exercise also makes many people feel more positive and confident which is likely to be helpful in renewing your love life.

Diabetics who are taking drugs or insulin to control the condition should seek expert advice before beginning an exercise programme. There is no reason why a healthy young diabetic should not undertake a demanding exercise programme but it is necessary to reduce the insulin dose or eat some extra carbohydrate before vigorous exercise. When diabetes is controlled by diet or the drug metformin (Glucophage), no special precautions are required before exercise.

CHAPTER SEVEN:
the food of love

> It provokes the desire, but it takes away the
> performance. Therefore much drink may be said to
> be an equivocator with lechery
> Macbeth, XI:3
> **William Shakespeare (1564 - 1616)**

Fruit, vegetables and fish are the food of love. You should aim to eat at least five portions of fruit and vegetables a day. For example, you might eat an orange at breakfast time, an apple as a snack during the day, a portion of peas, a portion of lettuce and a tomato. A good plan is to eat fruit after meals instead of puddings or ice cream. Potatoes are starchy, and though they contribute some fibre and nutrients to the diet, they should not be counted as part of your five portions of fruit and vegetables. As well as fibre, vegetables give you essential vitamins and minerals which are important for maintaining the arteries in good condition and preventing cancer.

Fish is very beneficial to health, particularly oily fish such as salmon, mackerel, sardines, or herring. Try to eat fish at least once a week. Fish oils help to prevent the accumulation of atheroma which blocks arteries and causes so many problems with the circulation. Use vegetable oils such as soya oil, sunflower seed oil, rapeseed oil, or olive oil for cooking – avoid using butter, margarine and animal fat for cooking. Use brands of margarine that are high in polyunsaturated fats.

A diet with a lot of fat, particularly animal fat, results in fatty deposits of atheroma in blood vessels so reduce the amount of fat in your diet. Eat fewer cakes and biscuits – they contain a lot of fat and, because they are made of white flour, contain relatively few nutrients. Make wholemeal bread your first choice – it contains many more vitamins and vital minerals than white bread as well as being a valuable source of fibre. Limit the amount of cheese you eat and when you do eat cheese with bread or biscuits avoid putting on butter or margarine as well. Avoid eating cream and ice cream on a regular basis – make it a special treat – and use semi-skimmed milk.

You can also reduce the amount of fat in your diet by changing cooking methods: avoid fried foods – grill, bake, boil, poach, or steam instead. Trim visible fat from meat and avoid eating the skin of chicken. Use yogurt instead of cream. Avoid: wrapping food in pastry, deep frying in batter, thick sauces.

There is no need to worry about sugar unless you are eating large amounts. Sugary foods, especially biscuits and sweets, rot the teeth and contribute to overweight but sugar does not directly cause problems with the circulation. The danger of eating too many sweet foods is that they replace unprocessed foods such as fruit and vegetables in the diet. If you are having difficulty eating your five pieces of fruit and vegetables each day you should ask if you are eating too many sweet foods. Soft drinks contain a lot of sugar – cutting down on them can be a very effective way of losing weight.

Salt in the diet has been linked to high blood pressure so it is wise to limit the amount of salt in the diet. This is particularly important for men who are already suffering from high blood pressure. Reduce the amount of salt used in cooking and if possible avoid adding it at the table. Salt in food is an acquired taste. If you deliberately reduce the amount of salt in your diet you will find that you get used to eating food with very little salt. Bacon, cheese, salted nuts, and crisps are all better avoided by men who have a problem with high blood pressure. Fruit is a rich source of potassium which has the effect of dislodging salt (sodium) from the body – so it is particularly important for people with high blood pressure to eat fruit.

Lengthy books have been written on healthy eating. Here you have it in a few paragraphs. If you find it difficult or you need definite recipes or menu suggestions to work with you can obtain more information including recipes from the British Heart Foundation or the British Diabetic Association. (*For addresses, see page 105*)

overweight

People who are overweight are more likely to suffer from blood vessel disease, and so are more likely to have erection problems as well as a greater risk of heart disease. Men most at risk are those who have a lot of flesh around the middle. The risk of a heart attack has been found to be substantially increased for men who have a waist measurement of more than 40 inches. This risk can be reduced by losing weight.

When weight is lost symptoms of heart and blood vessel disease, such as angina and high cholesterol, are reduced.

Such observations suggest that improvement in erections can also be expected with loss of weight.

People who are overweight often have raised blood pressure. When they lose weight their blood pressure generally improves and may drop to normal levels. Men with high blood pressure who are able to maintain their weight loss often find that they can reduce their drugs or even stop them altogether. This is good news for men who have been taking blood pressure drugs that interfere with erections. Raised blood pressure is also linked to a greater risk of heart attacks, strokes and kidney disease so there is every reason for a man who is overweight and has high blood pressure to make a determined effort to lose weight. Heavy drinking can also cause raised blood pressure. *(See following section)*

At this point you must decide on priorities. Weight loss requires determination and motivation that some people find very difficult to raise. Your immediate aim is to regain good erections. You may well achieve this without going on a diet and without using drugs if you work hard on the pelvic floor exercises and/or use a constriction ring or a vacuum pump. If you are successful with these methods you may still consider losing weight in order to make a further gain in fitness and health – equally you may decide that it is not necessary or not a high priority.

If these non-drug methods of obtaining an erection do not produce a satisfactory result then the options are drugs, injections, or perhaps even an operation. At this point you may decide that a major effort to lose weight together with other body maintenance measures is worth trying. It is worth remembering that small gains in each of the important areas: weight loss, fitness, giving up smoking and reducing drinking may add up to a substantial gain in overall body function and bring the return of useful erections. But success cannot be guaranteed – and it may be that your blood vessel disease or diabetes has proceeded so far that improvement in health and fitness will be difficult.

However, even small improvements in fitness can be expected to help in achieving erection by drugs if you opt for that solution. And if drugs or injections do not work you can still, after careful thought, opt for an operation.

To lose weight successfully you must be prepared to alter eating habits one way or another. A good strategy is to begin by changing to the food of love (*see above*). Many people find that when they make a determined change to a low fat diet and cut down on alcohol and soft drinks they lose weight without too much difficulty. When your aim is to increase health and improve your chances of getting good erections, it is counter-productive to reduce weight by cutting down on the starchy foods such as bread, potatoes, pasta or rice. People who diet by cutting down on starchy foods inevitably end up eating more meat, eggs, cheese and other fatty foods. They may succeed in losing weight but at the same time they increase the proportion of fat in the diet which is bad for blood vessels – and erections.

Increasing the amount of exercise you take will help. A lot of diet books say that exercise uses up too few calories to make any difference. However, an increase in exercise produces a small increase in the number of calories burnt up by the body. It does not produce a dramatic weight loss immediately but may make a substantial difference in the long term.

Eating the food of love and introducing some exercise into your daily routine will take at least two or three weeks and it will take longer to make them a part of regular living. You must be careful not to try to change everything at once – go at a pace that you are able to sustain. Once you feel comfortable with a change to the food of love and have achieved an increase in exercise, however modest, you can start thinking about more direct ways of losing weight by dieting.

alcohol

Regular drinking of more than three alcoholic drinks a day has a number of adverse effects on the body (A pint of bitter or full-strength lager counts as two drinks, i.e, two units of alcohol). After many years of drinking at this rate a man's ability to obtain a good erection is likely to be reduced as well as his libido.

Regular drinking also stunts the normal growth of the testes so that they produce a much reduced quantity of male hormone. Furthermore, damage to the liver from drinking may cause an increase in production of the female hormone oestrogen. These two changes produce a reduction in masculine body type of hard-drinking men which may, for example, include reduced body hair but also a drastic reduction in the male libido.

Alcohol may also cause damage to nerves in many parts of the body and in particular nerves going to the penis which are necessary for erection. If consumption of alcohol is reduced before the damage is too extensive then a slow recovery of ability to have erections may be expected. However, even moderate consumption of alcohol may have a negative effect on erections, and improvement may then only be obtained with complete abstinence. One in four men drink more alcohol than is good for their health according to expert opinion. Men should not as a general rule drink more than three units of alcohol a day where one unit is a small glass of wine, a half pint of beer, or one pub measure of spirits. And they should aim to have two or three days a week either without alcohol – or with not more than one drink.

Drinking is a major cause of high blood pressure as well as erection difficulty. And high blood pressure is itself linked to erection problems because the drugs prescribed to reduce blood pressure may interfere with erections. High blood pressure may often be reduced to levels where drugs are no longer necessary by limiting alcohol to two units or less a day, losing five to 10 pounds in weight and restricting salt intake (Avoid adding salt in cooking and at table, avoid salty foods, and eat fewer prepared foods which contain added salt).

CHAPTER EIGHT:

Drug treatments

What potions have I drunk of Siren tears,
Distill'd from limbecks fooul as hell within
Sonnets
William Shakespeare (1564 - 1616)

New drug therapies have revolutionised the treatment of impotence. Injection treatment became widely available in the late 1980s and early 1990s. As a result it was recognised that impotence is often a physical problem and is susceptible to physical treatment.

Further progress is now being made with the discovery of new drugs and treatments which produce an erection without any need for an injection. One of these new treatments, MUSE, is available in the United States and is expected to become available in Britain before the end of 1997. Another drug, Viagra, will probably become generally available in Britain towards the end of 1998. Other new treatments are expected within two or three years.

These new methods of assisting erection will be much preferred by most men to an injection in the penis. Nevertheless these new treatments are not expected to completely replace injections which will continue to be used for some men who have more difficult erection problems.

New drugs for injection are also being developed and so it will become possible to treat some men who have previously not responded to treatment or had problems with existing injectables. Specialist doctors are also learning how to combine some drugs to produce treatments which enable erections to be obtained by men who would previously have had no alternative but surgery. Drugs may also be combined with use of a vacuum pump to help fill the penis with blood.

The simpler treatments, MUSE and Viagra, are likely to be available through GPs, or at least through GPs who take a specialist interest in erection problems.

Specialist clinics will also need to be set up for men with more complicated erection problems.These clinics should provide drugs and combination treatments together with counselling for those men and their partners who have special problems. Such specialist clinics do not exist in many areas at the time of writing and where they do exist may not be able to offer counselling and psychotherapy as well as physical treatments. Private clinics offering a range of treatments for impotence may be contacted through the yellow pages – be sure to ask about the cost of the consultation and the cost of drugs and compare prices before embarking on treatment.

As medical treatment of impotence becomes more efficient then the psychological side of the problem becomes more evident – and counselling or psychotherapy may be needed as well as drug treatment. Sometimes the man is willing but the woman is not and the couple need to talk through the problem with a counsellor. Sometimes a man provided with an artificial erection is too eager to proceed and does not appreciate the need for courtship of his partner. Once a man has a drug induced erection he may realise for the first time that he has another problem and is not keen to have intercourse despite the enthusiasm of his partner. Such problems need to be talked through with a counsellor. Counselling and sex therapy is available through a number of agencies. *(See page 104)*

Viagra – the 'Sex Pill'

Viagra is a tablet taken by mouth which may assist erection or make a man more sensitive to sexual arousal. When Viagra becomes available it is likely to become the treatment of first choice for impotence because it is so easy to take. GPs who do not want to prescribe a drug requiring injection (because they would have to instruct the patient in how to make the injection) may be less reluctant to prescribe Viagra once it has been cleared by drug approval authorities.

Viagra has been developed by Pfizer, the pharmaceutical company. Originally Pfizer intended the drug to be used for treatment of heart disease but researchers observed in early trials that men taking the drug had unwanted erections. Viagra (chemical name: sildenafil) works by enhancing relaxation of the corpora cavernosa, the cavities in the penis, allowing them to fill with blood in response to sexual stimulation. International scientific trials of Viagra by impotent men have found that it improves the frequency of erections as well the hardness and duration of erection. It enables intercourse to occur more frequently and more reliably in men who are impotent or who are unable to achieve intercourse as frequently as they and their partner wish.

Patients are advised to take Viagra about one hour before intercourse is anticipated. If they have had a heavy, fatty meal, the drug may take longer to work. Alternatively the drug may be taken on a daily basis in order to increase the possibility of a satisfactory erection when sexual excitement occurs. In trials of Viagra, partners of the men using the drug noted it was effective, as well as the men themselves. Trials have shown that men taking the drug have increased enjoyment of intercourse and increased satisfaction with their sex life compared with men taking a dummy drug. However trials have also shown that Viagra does not increase desire, that is the wish to have intercourse, beyond the normal level. Viagra acts as an enabler, making it easier for men with erectile difficulty to respond sexually.

Viagra has been found to work effectively in men who have diabetes and spinal cord injuries, as well as in men who have no known physical cause for their impotence. This suggests that the drug may be useful in the treatment of impotence which has a psychological basis, and particularly useful when there are psychological as well as physical reasons for impotence. No serious side effects of the drug have been observed in these trials. The most common side effects were headache, flushing and indigestion.

other drugs taken by mouth

Phentolamine taken by mouth has been used experimentally to induce erections with modest success rates of 30-40% in a group of men which included men with diabetes and circulation problems. The drug was either taken on a continuous basis over a period or placed between tongue and cheek for direct absorption 20-30 minutes before intercourse. Trazodone by mouth over a 30-day period has been used with 65% success in men who do not have known physical problems that might prevent erection. Pentoxifylline has been used over a 12-week period in a small group of men with 50% success. These treatments are all still experimental and cannot be recommended except when they are administered in a research setting with detailed supervision and follow-up.

Men whose erection problem is the result of arterial disease will almost certainly benefit by having their arterial disease treated by statins, drugs which have been shown to reduce fatal and non-fatal heart attacks and sudden death. The remarkable success of these drugs was first shown in a trial on men in the West of Scotland which goes under the name of WOSCOPS and a trial in Scandinavia which is known as the 4S trial. Many other trials have followed which show that statin drugs lower cholesterol and have a direct effect on atheroma, the substance that blocks arteries, stabilising it and improving the function of arteries.

MUSE (Medicated Urethral System for Erection)

MUSE makes use of an applicator to insert a drug pellet into the urethra – that is the tube in the penis through which urine is passed. The pellet releases the drug, alprostadil, which dissolves in the small amount of urine left in the penis. The drug is then absorbed into the penis as it is gently massaged. MUSE is already available in the United States and was expected to be available in Britain before the end of 1997. Two-thirds of men whose impotence is primarily a physical problem are able to achieve an erection using MUSE in the clinic. However some of these men experience difficulty using the system at home. About two-thirds of the men who succeed in getting an erection in the clinic are able to achieve an erection and satisfactory intercourse at home. Men who have satisfactory intercourse after using the system and continue to use it find that they can get a good erection on about seven out of ten occasions when they use it. The erection begins within five to ten minutes of inserting the pellet and generally lasts between 30-60 minutes.

Care must be taken to ensure that the pellet is inserted well into the urethra and is not dislodged and that the penis is fully massaged. It is important not to lie down immediately after insertion of the pellet as this reduces blood flow into the penis. Loveplay should continue with the man sitting up, standing, or walking.

Muse is available in four dosages and a higher dosage may be used if one of the lower dosages proves to be ineffective. You will probably need to try the drug out first under medical supervision to find out the best dosage for you and observe that there are no side effects. In some men MUSE has been found to cause a lowering of blood pressure and fainting. MUSE can be used twice in 24 hours.

A soft rubber constriction ring has been developed for use with MUSE. The ring stops blood from leaving the penis but is not sufficiently tight to stop it from filling with blood. The ring is helpful for men who find that they obtain some response with MUSE but not sufficient response to gain a hard or effective erection.

The most serious side effect of MUSE is prolonged rigid erections lasting four to six hours in 0.3% of men using the system and more rarely priapism, a rigid erection lasting longer than six hours *(see treatments for prolonged erections, below)*. These complications occur in a similar frequency with injection treatment. Priapism is treated as a medical emergency. It is relieved by a minor operation to withdraw some blood from the penis. Medical advice should be sought if an erection lasts more than four hours.

treatment of prolonged erections

A number of ways may be used to ease a prolonged erection and speed detumescence, that is encourage the penis to return to its normal relaxed state. Exercise in the form of brisk walking, running up and down stairs, or a work-out on an exercise bike are generally effective in reducing an unwanted erection. Prolonged erections may sometimes be relieved by application of ice packs to the inner thighs. The ice pack should be applied alternately to each inner thigh for a period not exceeding ten minutes. A drug called Sudafed, which does not require a prescription, has also been found to be helpful for the treatment of prolonged erections. These measures may be taken as soon as persistence of the erection becomes inconvenient. If an erection persists for more than three hours these steps should be taken anyway. An erection should not be allowed to persist for more than four hours because there is the possibility of damage to nerves if it continues. Contact your doctor or go to your nearest emergency department if your erection persists for four hours. The erection will easily be relieved by removal of a small amount of blood.

If a prolonged erection is obtained with MUSE a lower dose should be used or the method should not be used. Some men who suffer from sickle cell anaemia, sickle cell trait, leukaemia, or bone marrow tumours may be prone to prolonged erections and should not use MUSE or injection treatment.

Use of MUSE is also associated with a local ache or pain in the penis in about one-third of men. However, only about one in 10 men who choose the system for home use have pain in the penis. Partners sometimes experience some vaginal itching after having intercourse. This may be due to resumption of intercourse after a period of abstinence. Water based lubricants are generally helpful. If the problem persists medical advice should be sought. MUSE should not be used for sexual intercourse with a woman who is pregnant without use of a condom.

Use of decongestants, cold and allergy remedies, and appetite suppressant drugs may block the effect of MUSE and so should be avoided.

MUSE has been developed by Vivus, a US company based in Menlo Park, California, but is being marketed in Britain by another company, Astra.

Apomorphine

Apomorphine is a drug which is well-known to medicine. It has been used in the past mainly as an emetic, that is to induce vomiting. It causes a powerful feeling of nausea. This might seem to be an unpromising start for a drug which might be used to induce erections and the love-making that generally follows. However apomorphine can be combined with other drugs that control nausea and vomiting. Research is now going on to produce a drug combination including apomorphine that can be used for treatment of impotence. Apomorphine probably induces erections by increasing the level of certain chemical messengers such as dopamine in the brain. Although the way apomorphine works is not exactly understood it will probably be used together with drugs such as Viagra, which works by its local effect on the penis, or with injections in the penis. The combination of one drug working on the brain and another working locally in the penis may be expected to help some men when neither drug by itself is sufficient.

the discovery of injection erections

In the early 1980s Dr Ronald Virag, a Paris surgeon, was astounded when a patient who had been impotent had an erection while he was under anaesthetic on the operating table. Theatre staff were embarrassed, but Dr Virag realised that what they had witnessed was of major scientific and medical importance.

Dr Virag had been operating on the blood vessels around the man's penis and had injected a drug, papaverine, to dilate the man's arteries after the operation. If the drug could produce an erection under anaesthetic when there is no conscious erotic stimulus, then it might be used to help men with erection problems, reasoned Dr Virag. So he tried it out, very cautiously at first, as a test and as a way of exercising the penis.

At the same time another pioneer, Dr Giles Brindley, a British neurologist, specialising in spinal injuries discovered he could obtain erections in paralysed patients by injections in the penis. He made a dramatic demonstration of the technique on himself at a meeting of the American Association of Urologists in Las Vegas in 1983, so convincing the world that the technique worked.

Dr Virag and Dr Brindley had invented the injection erection. Dr Virag found that following these artificial erections in the clinic some patients were able to have better natural erections at home. Then some of the men asked him if they could make the injection at home themselves to induce an erection before intercourse. So Dr Virag taught some patients to inject themselves and encouraged them to take the drug at home where they were able to make the injection just before intercourse.

The injection has revolutionised the treatment and diagnosis of impotence. It has been particularly helpful for men who have difficulty in obtaining erections because of accidental damage to the spine – and for men who suffer from acute anxiety about obtaining an erection. Some men have been able to have families as a result of this new technique. Many more have been able to keep together marriages which were falling apart because the wife believed that she was unloved.

treatment using injections

Robert, a Londoner aged 67, was one of the first men in Britain to benefit from the new injection treatment. Robert married a wife who is much younger than him. She wanted to have a baby but he found that he was unable to have satisfactory intercourse. He was taking drugs for treatment of diabetes and high blood pressure. His doctor adjusted his drugs and he was able to get a better erection but it was still not strong enough for penetration. Robert's doctor then told him about injection treatment. He tried it and the injection produced a hard erection which enabled him to have intercourse. When he and his wife decided that they wanted to make love Robert would go to the bathroom to inject himself. Then they would wait around 15 minutes or so while the injection took effect.

"I injected a little bit nervously at first," said Robert. "But it worked and I learnt how to handle it better. At first I worried a bit about how long the erection would last but I needn't have. Sometimes it would take three hours to go down."

Until Robert had the injection treatment he had not been able to have full intercourse with his wife. He and his wife have not yet been able to conceive a child but being able to consummate their marriage has made them very happy. "It has brought us closer together. We understand each other better now," said Robert.

Men vary in the size and firmness of erection induced by injection and the same man may vary from one occasion to the next. This is because the strength of the erection also varies with the strength of the erotic stimulus and the man's reaction to it – and these vary between one time and the next. With experience the dose of drug can be adjusted to produce an erection which generally goes down soon after intercourse. However, men who use the injection treatment are all warned that an erection may sometimes last longer than is convenient (priapism). If an erection lasts longer than four hours there is a danger of damage to nerves, although one man who was caught short flew from London to New York by Concorde with a full erection. When an erection lasts longer than four hours it is advisable to have hospital treatment to reduce the erection by removal of blood. (*See panel, page 56*)

Mr Gordon Williams, a urologist at Hammersmith Hospital, London, warns that injections are not a simple answer to erection problems: "All the injections do is produce an erection. Sex therapy and psychotherapy have an important role and need to be done in conjunction with injections for the majority of men."

Initially, the drugs most commonly used for injection in the penis were papaverine and phentolamine. However these drugs can be rather irritating to local tissues and have been associated with fibrosis – small lumps that form near the point of injection. Use of these drugs has been largely replaced by prostaglandin E1 (Caverject) because it is not so irritating. Some doctors continue to use papaverine and phentolamine because they are cheaper. In September 1997 another drug, Erecnos, became available and it appears to be a further improvement.

A lot of men have problems with the idea of injection in such a sensitive area – even when they understand that the injection is in the shaft of the penis which is relatively insensitive. Some men feel dizzy or faint following the injection and this may be because they are sensitive to the drug or that they are reacting psychologically. Faintness is not generally a problem for men who persist with the method.

Various quite different results have been obtained with injection therapy. Dr Virag, who sometimes has prescribed a mixture of drugs for injection, has reported an 85 per cent success rate with injections. However in other series of patients, for example those studied at the State University of New York Health Science Center, only one in four men who tried the injection method were still using it six months later.

Most of the others obtained satisfactory erections and were able to have intercourse, but seemed to decide that the method did not suit them. Many of the men said that they would have continued if the same result could be achieved without an injection. Some were older men who had become accustomed to a life without sex and found it comfortable to return to a more undemanding way, some had physical difficulty in making the injections and had a partner who was unable or unwilling to help with the injection. Those who dropped out also included some successes. A number of men stopped the injections because normal erections returned.

Erecnos has made injections easier and overcome some of the problems *(see below)*. Nevertheless injection treatment is now likely to be reserved for men who do not respond to MUSE or other drugs which do not involve injection.

Caverject

Injections of prostaglandin E1 (brand name Caverject) have been the standard treatment for a number of years because prostaglandin is not so irritating as papaverine and phentolamine. However there is now competition from Erecnos, MUSE, and other drugs. In a typical trial of Caverject 70 per cent of a group of men with various erection problems had a full erection maintained for at least 30 minutes. The erection began on average seven and a half minutes after the injection and lasted an average of almost two and half hours.

Caverject is considerably more expensive than papaverine and phentolamine but it has the advantage that prolonged erections (priapism) are relatively less frequent. Erections lasting more than three hours occur occasionally in about one per cent of patients using Caverject, and, in one in a thousand men, are so prolonged that emergency treatment is necessary. The manufacturers, Upjohn, say that priapism may be avoided by not using more than one injection in a 24-hour period and not using more than three injections a week. *(See panel page 56 for treatment of prolonged erections)*

Bruises commonly occur at the site of injection in the penis but these are not uncomfortable and do not cause any long-term problems. The risk of formation of fibrous lumps at the site of injection in the penis is also less with Caverject and so papaverine and phentolamine are now used comparatively seldom. About one in six men report a continuous dull ache in the penis after injection but this pain is not sufficiently great to prevent intercourse in men who are well-motivated. However, some men found the pain distracting and gave it as a reason for not continuing with injections.

Injection treatment will be increasingly reserved for men who do not respond to drugs such as Viagra or MUSE. In future injections are likely to be used in combination with these drugs for men who have the greatest difficulty in achieving erections. Doctors are finding that some men who do not respond to the injection of a single drug do respond if a mixture of drugs are injected.

New drugs are also being developed for use as injectables for inducing erection. These include a hormone known as VIP, or vaso-intestinal peptide, and Erecnos. The advantage of these drugs is said to be that they are less likely to induce prolonged erections lasting more than four hours.

Erecnos

Erecnos produces erection within 10 minutes of injection and is said by the manufacturers, the French drug company Fournier, to give a more natural erection than is achieved with prostaglandin E1 or with a vacuum pump. When Erecnos is compared with other drugs in trials Fournier has found that there is less risk of pain at the injection site and less risk of prolonged erections. If this experience is borne out by doctors in everyday practice then Erecnos is likely to become the first choice for injection treatment.

In one trial of Erecnos between 64 and 73 per cent of men using the drug reported that they had an erection which was adequate for intercourse. Two-thirds of men's partners said that they were satisfied with the intercourse. Pain at the site of the injection occurred in less than one per cent of men who injected themselves with Erecnos. Erecnos is also more convenient because it is supplied in a ready-to-use syringe.

Erecnos is described medically as an alpha1 blocker. It blocks nerve signals in the penis enabling the penis to relax and fill with blood. Prolonged erections occurred in only 0.1% of patients using Erecnos and these patients were able to continue using a smaller dose of the drug without problems.

More than 80 per cent of men using Erecnos had a return of spontaneous erections or an improvement in spontaneous erections. Two-thirds of the men who discontinued the drug after a period of successful use were able to maintain satisfactory sexual activity without it.

Invicorp

Invicorp is a combination of a hormone known as VIP, or vaso-intestinal peptide, and phentolamine. It is in late stage development by a company called Senetek and is expected to become available for prescription sometime in 1998. Invicorp has been found to be safe and effective in trials but details are not yet available. Invicorp is available in an automatic injector for virtually painless delivery of the drug.

Like Erecnos, Invicorp will have advantages for some men and is expected not to induce prolonged erections so frequently as first generation drugs.

future developments

Men who have not been able to achieve regular or satisfactory erections with Caverject or Erecnos may in future be treated with combinations of drugs. One of these mixtures, called Trimix, containing prostaglandin E1, papaverine and phentolamine, has proved to be particularly effective. It has been widely used in the United States although it is not licensed for injection in the penis. It is less painful than prostaglandin E1 alone because a smaller volume of liquid is injected. Other mixtures are likely to be developed for men who have special difficulty. Injections may also be combined with a tablet given by mouth or with use of a vacuum pump in the future.

hormone replacement therapy for men

It sounds like a great idea – replace the missing hormones in aging men and their normal sexual energy, including ability to obtain a firm erection, will return. Hormone replacement therapy appears to work for many women – so why shouldn't it work for men too?

Masters and Johnson made the classic studies of decline in sexual response with age. They found that erection is delayed in older men. Young men may achieve an erection within a few seconds whereas some minutes of stimulation may be necessary to produce an erection in a man in his 50s or 60s. However, when older men reach what Masters and Johnson called the plateau phase of intercourse they are often able to prolong it more easily than a younger man. As a result the female partner has more time to reach orgasm and older men gain a reputation as accomplished lovers.

If ejaculation were a suitable measure of sexual ability then older men certainly show a decline in power. Older men may only eject their semen a distance of three inches to a foot whereas a younger man may eject semen a distance of up to two feet. In older men the erection may be lost very rapidly after intercourse, and it may be several hours, or even days, before an older man is able to obtain another erection and attempt intercourse again, whereas the younger man may have another erection within minutes. Often an older man will be able to obtain an erection which is firm enough for intercourse once or twice a week but be unable to regularly achieve orgasm and ejaculate.

Doctors have argued over the years whether there is a such a thing as the male menopause, sometimes called the andropause. The male hormone, testosterone, declines in quantity in the blood with age but there is no obvious point in men, equivalent to the cessation of ovulation, that might mark the start of a male menopause. Testosterone plays a crucial role in the development of the male body from the time when the baby boy is developing in the womb through adolescence, but its role in later life is not well understood. It is widely believed to be concerned with erection and ejaculation as well as with masculine libido, temperament, and emotional response. However, the majority of men still have enough testosterone in their blood when they are in their 60s and 70s to keep the male organs at least ticking over. Symptoms such as fatigue, depression, irritability and reduction in sex drive are blamed on the andropause, but these symptoms occur in men of all ages and are all too common in middle-aged men who have normal testosterone levels.

Doctors concerned with erection problems generally measure the amount of testosterone in a patient's blood as part of a full clinical work up. And when the blood level of testosterone is significantly below normal they do not hesitate to prescribe extra. In such cases the treatment is generally considered to be very effective. However prescription of testosterone for middle-aged and older men who have a normal level of testosterone for their age, albeit lower than that of a young man, has not been shown to be an effective way of improving erections long term. Nevertheless testosterone is often prescribed by private doctors and clinics for older men because of its powerful psychological effect. A man who is told to take testosterone is usually impressed with what he sees as the potential of the treatment and goes away determined to test his virility. However such enthusiasm does not generally last long – and for a man with a real erection problem testosterone is likely to act only as a source of frustration.

There have been few, if any, adequate scientific studies of whether giving testosterone improves erections. One study has gone further than others and shown that male hormone treatment does not improve erections in men with normal levels of the hormone in their blood , although it did increase their interest in sex (*R.O'Carroll, J.Bancroft. Testosterone therapy for low sexual interest and erectile dysfunction in men: a controlled study. Br. J.Psych 1984, vol 145, pp 146-151*). Prescription of testosterone to a man with erection problems will generally only increase frustration – it will make them more interested in sexual activity but no more able to accomplish the act.

Testosterone may be provided in a number of different ways. A popular new way of providing it is as a patch which can be applied to the skin. The patch, called Andropatch, is put on at night over an area of muscle. The advantage of this method is that the drug reaches a peak in the blood in the mornings, mimicking the natural daily variation of testosterone in the blood. However the patch can cause skin irritation. Alternatives are: a daily tablet, injections every three to four weeks, or an implant that lasts about six months. Peak levels occur in the blood immediately after the injection or implantation of the drug and decline thereafter. Thus many men find a daily tablet or patch is generally preferable.

Some men who have a borderline deficiency of testosterone find that one course of treatment restores their sexual capability and they can then continue without further medication. Testosterone treatment should not be undertaken unless it is really necessary because the hormone may stimulate early development of prostate cancer which is a common disease in older men.

About five men in a thousand are deficient in testosterone. The most common cause is Klinefelter's syndrome which occurs in 1.5 out of 1000 live male births. Other causes are viral infections of the testes, alcohol abuse, injury or surgical removal of both testes. Testosterone deficiency may also be caused by a tumour of the pituitary gland.

The main signs and symptoms of testosterone deficiency after puberty are reduced energy and vitality, reduced interest in sex and little or no sexual urge, difficulty in getting erections, loss of body hair and reduction in growth of facial hair, reduction in normal loss of hair on the head, depression and mood changes. Signs which may be found on medical investigation are anaemia and low sperm production. Replacement of testosterone restores mood and improves sexual function and erections in men who have a genuine deficiency of this hormone.

Male kidney dialysis patients often have problems with erection. Dialysis may remove testosterone from the body. However correction of low testosterone levels is not very effective in restoring capability for erections, according to a study undertaken by Dr Ian Lawrence at Leicester Royal Infirmary. Vacuum pumps were found to be a much more reliable way of restoring erections and sexual capability.

CHAPTER NINE:
erections assisted with a pump

Sex is one of the nine reasons for reincarnation...
the other eight are unimportant
Big Sur and the Oranges of Hieronymus Bosch
Henry Miller (1891 - 1980), American novelist

Many men who have had problems in obtaining or maintaining an erection have found that pumps are very helpful. Pumps work in some men who do not respond to drugs or injections. Some men prefer pump systems because it gives them full control and avoids the need to take any kind of drug.

To obtain an erection using this method a plastic cylinder is put over the penis and air is withdrawn from it with a pump, creating a partial vacuum. The vacuum gradually draws blood up into the penis. It generally takes one or two minutes (exceptionally up to five minutes) for the penis to become fully engorged with blood – then a specially-designed elastic band is slipped over the base of the penis. This prevents the blood from draining away and returning to the body.

In the majority of men who use this method the "vacuum erection" reaches much the same length and circumference as a normal erection. However, it is not an entirely normal erection and sensation for the man may not be exactly the same as with a normal erection. Even so the erection allows satisfying intercourse for both partners.

The vacuum device was invented at least 80 years ago but was not widely available until the 1970s. Now such devices are much better known and have been extensively tested by the medical profession. Different brands are available varying in price from about £120 to £300. At the upper end of the price range is the Erecaid which uses a patent elastic ring with grooves on the inside edge. These grooves allow some blood flow during erection. So if the ring is accidentally left in position for a long period the penis will not be damaged through lack of oxygen.

The Erecaid device was tested by Dr Philip Wiles at the General Infirmary, Leeds, in 1988. Ten diabetic men with an average age of 55 were instructed in the use of the device. All achieved a lasting erection with it and none experienced any unpleasant side effects. Nine of the 10 men used the device satisfactorily – one man did not test it fully at home because of marital disharmony. The men varied in their enthusiasm but gave their erections an average seven out of 10. Their partners also varied in their response but also rated their satisfaction on average as seven out of 10. Dr Wiles concluded that it was a safe, simple and effective method of managing erection difficulty. The Erecaid is provided with either a manually or a battery-operated pump. *(See panel page 74 for further details)*

Another vacuum device the "Active", from a different manufacturer, has also been evaluated at Leeds. Eleven out of 19 diabetic men who tested it continued to use it for more than six months and had intercourse about once a week on average. They rated the device as highly-effective and painless in use, and they found that ejaculation was satisfactory despite the constriction ring. Three patients reported that their natural ability to obtain and sustain an erection was restored after using the device and they no longer needed to use it. It may be that use of the device helps to restore normal blood flow in the penis – or that the device, by providing a 100 per cent reliable erection, restores confidence to men who had come to believe that their ability to have an erection had gone forever. *(See panel on pages 74-75 for details)*

Some men who use constriction devices find that they do not ejaculate satisfactorily and may feel that the experience is incomplete. The constriction ring may inhibit ejaculation but many men are able to ejaculate satisfactorily with it in position. A possible reason for absence of ejaculation is a tendency to reduce or neglect foreplay when the erection is achieved by external means. In any case it is always wise to remember not to hurry love-making when using an external means to achieve erection. At the beginning when a couple is unfamiliar with the new device, anxiety may cause love-making to be hurried.

At the start of a new relationship when a couple first starts to make love they often feel a bit clumsy and do not know how best to satisfy each other. It is likely to be the same for some couples who start using the vacuum device. They must learn the best way of incorporating it into a way of loving which works well for both partners. Where direct comparisons have been made partners have generally found pumps no more awkward than injections. Most women report significant increases in their sexual arousal and satisfaction. However some women have commented that the penis feels cold when erection has been achieved with the help of a pump. This may be minimised by keeping the bedroom warm.

Vacuum devices and injections in the penis have been compared by a team from the Department of Urology at the University of California. They considered that the vacuum devices proved to be better than injections in a number of situations. When a man is alcoholic or has liver problems, has severe blood vessel disease, or has had an implant in the

suppliers of vacuum pumps and constriction rings

Suppliers of genuine quality pumps designed for regular long term use are listed with their principle products below. Avoid cheap pumps which are advertised by sex shops as penis exercisers and the like. They are not effective and cannot be recommended. Cheap models of this type examined by the author were not supplied with constriction rings and could only be made to work with considerable difficulty.

The quality pumps from suppliers listed below vary a great deal in the convenience and sophistication of their design – and in price. Some electrical pumps are available which at first seem as if they might be more convenient. However electrical pumps cannot be generally recommended because they are noisy, sometimes less reliable, and do not provide the sensitive control that can be obtained with a hand pump. Nevertheless electrical pumps may have an advantage for a man who has arthritis or is otherwise disabled.

Choose a one-piece cylinder and pump which can easily be operated with only one hand. Constriction rings are sold with pumps as part of a kit and are also sold as separate items for men who are able to get a satisfactory erection but lose it quickly. A selection of rings of different sizes is desirable so that you can choose a ring which is both comfortable and effective.

Prices given were correct at the time of publication but may have changed so it is advisable to check before ordering. Suppliers will send details of their products and price lists on request. VAT is not payable on medical supplies for personal use. If you are not satisfied with the product and return it soon after purchase some suppliers will refund much of the price.

penis which subsequently had to be removed the vacuum method works better than injections. On the other hand men who have certain blood diseases (dyscrasias), are using anticoagulant therapy, or have mild Peyronie's disease (a bend in the penis) may find injections more suitable.

The obvious first choice for most couples is between a drug taken by mouth such as Viagra, the MUSE system, and a vacuum pump. The most important consideration for most

---

For those men who want a cheap but reliable pump the Impower VTS device can be recommended. Currently it sells for £117.00 + £6.00 p&p from Impower Ltd 107 The Broadway, Mill Hill, London NW7 3TG.

Osbon Medical (UK), 107 The Broadway, Mill Hill, London NW7 3TG, offer a clinical demonstration of all their devices as well as a free telephone counselling service on: 0181 906 0777. This company is a pioneer in the field and has a reputation for quality pumps through the price range. Several models of pump are available costing from £145.00 to £320.00 for the electrical model, p&p £6.00. StayErec constriction rings and loading cone are available for £50.00 for a set of four rings providing two sizes and two tensions.

Eurosurgical Ltd, Merrow Business Centre, Guildford GU4 7WA, tel: 01483 456007 offer three pumps at prices from £120.00 + to £248.00 for a battery operated pump, £8.65 p&p. Their ring constriction device costs £69.00 + p&p, and provides four sizes of rings.

Genesis Medical Ltd, Freepost WD 1242, London NW3 4YR. Helpline: 0171 284 2824. Impulse pump device, £119.00, requires two hands for operation. Active II pump device £149.00. Asset – a ring constriction device with five rings of different sizes – price: £24.00

Owen Mumford Ltd, Medical Shop, Freepost, Woodstock, Oxon, OX20 1BR, tel: 01993 812021 provide a rapport VTD pump at £119.00. Recommended by Which, the Consumer's Association magazine, for good value and ease of use. The pump can be operated with one hand but takes a longer time to establish a vacuum than most other pumps. Constriction ring loading system at £19.95 is cheap but only two sizes of ring are offered.

men will be comfort, convenience, and how natural the method is. Some men will find that a pill or the MUSE system is more natural because once the drug is taken or inserted in the penis intercourse is normal, whereas the vacuum method requires the wearing of a constriction ring which some men find uncomfortable, distracting, or embarrassing.

Men who prefer the vacuum method say that they like to be able to initiate loveplay without an erection and that prior loveplay assists in obtaining a good erection with the pump. Couples who are able to bring use of the pump into loveplay have most success with it.

A further advantage of the pump is that men with psychological difficulties seem to be able to transfer easily from use of the pump to normal erection, whereas men with a psychological problem who use injections, for example, seem to become more dependent on them.

Another advantage of the vacuum erection method is that it does not need any elaborate medical diagnosis before it is tried out. It is wise to consult a doctor to see if there is any unrecognised medical reason for the erection difficulty such as diabetes, high blood pressure, or heart disease. It is helpful to have a consultation with someone familiar with use of the pump. But a complicated medical work-up and return visits to the doctor are not necessary.

Vacuum devices may be combined with the use of a drug or injection if none of these methods is entirely satisfactory when used alone. This combination approach has helped men who would not otherwise be able to obtain a useful erection. When the pump is used together with an injection care should be taken to wait for about 10 minutes after the injection before using the pump in order to allow time for the drug to act and to avoid bruising at the site of injection.

a word of warning: *Attempts to use a vacuum cleaner to induce erection may cause serious damage to the penis. The suction is much too powerful so it is extremely unwise to attempt to obtain an erection in this way. The suction from the purpose-built pumps discussed above is gentle and will not cause any harm.*

CHAPTER TEN:
surgical operations

Is sex necessary?
Title of a book
**James Thurber and E.B. White (1894-1961 and
1899 -), American writers, humorists and
cartoonists**

When the penis does not respond sufficiently to pelvic floor
exercises, vacuum constriction devices, drugs or injections,
then surgery may be considered as an option. However, so
many new drug treatments are now becoming available that
surgery cannot be recommended at the present time except
in the most difficult cases. Doctors are learning how best to
use the new drugs in combination to overcome the more
difficult problems. Men who do not respond to injections
should consider asking for combination drug treatment. The
possibilities are a mixture of drugs for injection, a
combination of a drug taken by mouth with injections, and a
combination of all or some of these with use of a pump.

Various types of surgical operation are available. However,
these operations are not easy to obtain through the National
Health Service and are expensive if obtained privately.

operation to improve arterial supply

Arteries may become partially blocked as a result of an
accident of some kind or by atheroma, a deposit in the walls
of arteries which is increased by smoking and a diet high in
animal fats. Men who have problems with arterial supply to

the penis may also have other conditions such as pain on walking caused by a poor blood supply to the legs (intermittent claudication), and angina which is caused by a poor supply of blood to the coronary arteries. Men with these problems may be able to prevent or delay worsening of their condition by giving up smoking and making some simple changes in diet (*see the food of love, page 43*). Statin drugs which have been shown to stabilise and even reduce atheroma and to prolong life may be indicated for men with these problems. Statin drugs might also be expected to have beneficial effects on the arterial supply to the penis.

Operations which attempt to bypass areas of blockage in arteries leading to the penis can be very successful in some patients generally those whose problem stems from accidental damage, but these operations are not so successful when the blockage is a result of arterial disease. Another operation which involves joining an artery directly to a vein in the penis has been reported to achieve better results in some patients. These are highly-specialised operations which may be obtained through the National Health Service by younger men who have suffered accidental damage. The way to find out more about them is by being referred to a hospital consultant specialising in urology. Other means of solving the problem such as drugs and injections should be tried first. It is worth trying the pelvic floor exercise because often there is some leakage as well as a problem in blood supply and the exercises may produce improvement. The vacuum pump will often prove to be helpful for men with a problem of arterial blood supply to the penis.

operation to prevent "venous leakage"

Some men respond to the injection of stimulating drugs into the penis with just a brief erection. The reason for this in some cases is that the blood leaks out of the penis returning through veins into the body. Operations are available which aim to seal this "venous leakage", or "veno-occlusive dysfunction" as it is now called. Several types of venous leakage have been identified and some respond well to surgery while others do not. In selected patients the success of the procedure on short-term follow up varies from 20 to 70 per cent – on follow-up a year later, success is generally about 25%. The variation in success probably depends as much on the selection of patients as on the particular merits of the surgeon and the technique. Men who respond best to this operation are non-smokers under 50 with no evidence of general arterial disease and a definite leak identified by colour Doppler diagnosis.

Surgery to the penis carries a small risk of reduced penile sensation, scarring, and shortening as well as the usual risks of a major operation involving a general anaesthetic. Shortening need not be a serious worry since length of the penis does not affect sensation for the partner. It is not that "size does not matter" – as is often said. Size does matter – but it is width not length that matters. Some women find it difficult to achieve an orgasm during intercourse if the penis is very slim.

Except for a few men who have unusually large veins around the penis or unusual anatomy of the veins in that area an operation should be the last choice. As explained in the section on pelvic floor exercises Belgian surgeons have found that these exercises produce a result which is as good as this type of surgery. So the exercises and other non-invasive methods, such as drugs, constriction rings and vacuum pump, should be tried first over a period of months before opting for surgery, which in any case is not easy to obtain on the National Health Service.

implants

Operations to insert a plastic rod into the penis to stiffen it have been in use now for at least 30 years and have proved to be remarkably popular. They have now been superseded to a large extent by new drugs, and by the injection and vacuum constriction methods of obtaining an erection which are less invasive. As with the other operations outlined in the preceding section this operation should not be considered until non-invasive methods such as drugs, pelvic floor exercises, vacuum constriction and injections have been tried or considered.

Nevertheless implants remain a valuable treatment for men who do not respond to other therapies. Several different types of plastic rods, called implants or protheses, are available. The simplest (the malleable prosthesis) consists of a plastic rod which bends at the base so the penis can be, as it were, hinged down for concealment and up for intercourse. Satisfactory intercourse can be achieved with this implant but the penis, although rigid, remains the same length and width which is a disadvantage.

A more elaborate inflatable implant is available which makes use of a small pump placed in the scrotum and a fluid reservoir in the abdomen. The pump is worked with finger and thumb sending fluid into two cylinders in the shaft of the penis. This has the advantage that the penis increases in width as well as in length and there is some evidence that partners find it more satisfying. The implant can be deflated at the press of a button. Even with this inflatable device the length of the penis stays much the same after the device is deflated.

An implant is worth considering when all other methods prove to be unhelpful. Men like Bobby Roberts, who suffers from severe diabetes, have a poor blood supply to the extremities of the body including the penis. Injection treatment and other methods will not work for them. Bobby who lives in Cantonment, Florida, was in his late twenties and had only been married for two years when his diabetes became worse and he started to find he could not obtain a satisfactory erection. His wife, Miki, believed that he had a girl friend and they began to lead separate lives. In fact Bobby was just spending more time with his friends while Miki worked 60 hours a week to take her mind off her worries.

At first Bobby and Miki weren't able to talk about the problem and they both became very distressed. Bobby said: "You feel like you're not really a full man, or like something without any sexuality at all. It really works on your nerves and your mind and it is something you think about full time." Bobby offered Miki a divorce. "But I said no, we've done this for better or for worse," said Miki. Then Bobby's doctor suggested he consider having an implant. Bobby was one of the first men to be given an inflatable penile implant, a device invented by Dr Brantley Scott in Houston, Texas. After Bobby had the implant he and Miki gradually got to know each other again and decided that they wanted a baby. So Bobby Jnr was conceived.

Miki says that their love life is now as good as it ever was, if not better. "You can pump it up and you can't do that naturally," she said. "The wives of men who have the implant say that their sex life is better than ever for that reason."

Many thousands of these implants have been inserted in the United States where they have been remarkably successful. However, there are complications in a minority of cases – up to one in 10 men using the implants meet problems. Sometimes the implants are uncomfortable, sometimes infections develop around them and sometimes they perforate the skin. In the case of the inflatable device the hydraulics sometimes fail and a second operation is necessary to repair the plumbing. Satisfaction with implants has been around 75 per cent.

Careful consideration needs to be given to whether or not an implant might be suitable. As with all methods of assisting erection greater success has been obtained when partners are involved in the decision making. When a partner is not involved then an implant may ruin what has been a good relationship by suddenly changing expectations. Some women are perfectly content with, or even prefer, a partner who is unable to have intercourse because they do not want to be sexually involved.

Insertion of an implant destroys much of the normal spongy

tissue of the penis that acts as a blood reservoir. So normal erections are not usually possible once an implant has been inserted. When insertion of an implant is unsuccessful, perhaps because of infection, it may have to be removed. In a few cases it is still possible to obtain an erection using a vacuum device. In fact satisfaction of partners is generally greater with vacuum or injection erections and so an implant should be the last option that is considered.

In theory implants are available in Britain through the National Health Service but the fact that men do not die when they are unable to have an erection and do not become ill in the usual sense of the word means that operations to insert penile implants are given little or no priority. The expense of the devices, which cost upwards of £500 each (excluding the cost of the operation) mean that even when the operation is available numbers are limited artificially. Relatively few men in the UK who might benefit from this operation are ever told about it and so few get the opportunity to have it. Doctors and administrators who are increasingly taking decisions about priorities put this type of operation at the bottom of the queue for resources. Nevertheless it is available on the National Health Service from a few specialist centres.

CHAPTER ELEVEN:
special problems

The pleasure is momentary, the position is ridiculous and the expense damnable
The Earl of Chesterfield (1694 - 1773), English statesman

ejaculation

Many men who have overcome erection difficulties using the methods described in this book have gone on to father children. Some men however, particularly men who are disabled by spinal injuries, cannot ejaculate normally or have difficulty in doing so – even though they are able to have an erection and accomplish the act of sexual intercourse.

There are a number of possible reasons for failure to ejaculate. Men who are using a constriction ring may feel that this is preventing or inhibiting ejaculation. The Erecaid ring has a "groove" which is said to make ejaculation easier and may be an advantage over other rings when a couple wish to conceive. Another possibility is that insufficient time is being spent on preliminary loveplay. The period of foreplay is important for the arousal of men as well as women. Tension builds up in the whole genital region during foreplay and the reservoirs and ducts which hold and carry the male genital secretions become toned up and ready to squirt out the seminal fluid. When erection is achieved by mechanical means, insufficient time may be given to this opening loveplay which is essential for ejaculation. If there is difficulty with ejaculation and a couple want to conceive, it is worth spending more time on loveplay as a first step.

Some men who have damage to nerves because of accidental injury, diabetes, or damage resulting from an operation, may not be able to ejaculate normally. Some ejaculate "backwards" into the bladder (called retrograde ejaculation) instead of through the penis. When this occurs it may still be possible with specialist help to rescue the sperm and use them for artificial insemination. Men who do not ejaculate at all can often be induced to ejaculate by electrical stimulation and can then father children but again specialist help is required. Couples with these problems should contact SPOD. (*Sexual and Personal Relationships of Disabled People, see page 105*)

love-making and the disabled

Disabled men, particularly those with spinal injuries, may have a number of special problems in love-making. After a serious injury it takes time to get to know your body once more – to understand any limitations and rediscover your sexuality. Your emotions may be much the same as they were before the injury but the ability to feel sensation in the genital area, to achieve an erection and to ejaculate may have been affected.

If your injury is incomplete you may still be able to achieve an erection as a result of psychological excitement, but if the injury is complete messages are unable to travel down from the brain to the genital area. An erection can then only be achieved by direct stimulation of the penis and genitals. If the injury is in the lower part of the spinal chord (below T10) then your ability to have an erection or to ejaculate may be affected. If the injury is complete then orgasms may be felt as little more than a tingling sensation in the groin but with incomplete injuries orgasm may still be a powerful experience, although it may be different from before. However, wherever the injury, love-making is still possible.

In hospital you have to get used to nurses putting in urinary catheters and helping you with bladder and bowel care. It may take time to reclaim your body and begin to feel it is your own again and that you are free to become sexually aroused. You will have to re-explore your body and find out once more what you can do with it and how.

Erection, orgasm and ejaculation may all seem impossible at first but when injury is incomplete these may return with practice and with help. The various methods of assisting erection described in this book may be helpful but should be discussed with your specialist medical adviser. Love-making without an erection is also possible *(see page 31)*. Oral sex is often a particularly successful way of love-making for disabled people especially if there is any difficulty in using the hands. More information about love-making and the disabled is available from SPOD. *(See page 105)*

Men with multiple sclerosis or spinal injury who do not ejaculate can often be induced to do so by stimulation with a special vibrator – and many have become fathers using this method. A vibrator designed for this purpose is available from Osbon Medical *(see address page 75)* and costs £350. Hospital spinal units are all equipped with the device where it may be tried and may be lent out for home use. It is quite different from the vibrators (dildos) available in sex shops which are designed for women. After using the special vibrator insemination can be achieved by a couple at home without medical help.

Men with high injuries above T6 have to take special care because they may develop a dangerous condition after orgasm or ejaculation known as autonomic dysreflexia which occurs as a dramatic and potentially life-threatening rise in blood pressure. This may be controlled by taking the drug Nifedipine beforehand.

Other electrical devices which stimulate the seminal vesicles via a probe inserted into the anus are available. This type of device may work if a vibrator has not been successful but it is only used as part of a hospital procedure. Couples with these problems should contact SPOD for more information. *(See page 105)*

CHAPTER TWELVE:
aphrodisiacs: do they work?

Better is a dinner of herbs where love is,
than a stalled ox and hatred therewith
Proverbs 15:13

The idea of a magical potion which will induce love, or at least increase sexual desire or performance, is common in literature. Drugs reputed to have such an effect are called aphrodisiacs. Various drugs referred to in this book will trigger erection and may increase susceptibility to sexual arousal in men and some might even have a similar effect in women. It is possible that certain herbs, which are reputed to have an aphrodisiac action, work in a similar way to these drugs. Indeed pioneering work in King Saud University in Riyadh, Saudi Arabia, is beginning to show that some traditional aphrodisiacs induce erection and mating behaviour in rats.

However engorgement of the sexual organs with blood is only a part of the process of sexual arousal – the mind must also be engaged if the process is to be fully completed. No drug has yet been shown to work this kind of magic.

A variety of products which claim to have aphrodisiac properties are sold in health food shops and by mail order through sex magazines. It is possible that some of these preparations have a direct or indirect effect on the reproductive urge, but some, probably most, work simply because men, or women, believe in them. Aphrodisiacs have a powerful placebo effect – that is whatever effect they have is increased because the man or woman taking the potion believes that it will work. A person who believes in a love potion of this kind has more confidence and more determination to try and so is more likely to succeed when it comes to seduction.

Doctors since time immemorial have used placebos, all sorts of concoctions from coloured water to snake oil, as a means of giving patients the idea that they are being helped by medical expertise. Dummy medicines mobilise the patients' enthusiasm and will to succeed, and so patients persuade themselves that their problem is going away, and when it comes to sex they try harder. The improvement in performance which results is usually attributed to the medicine when it may be entirely due to a person's freshly-stimulated enthusiasm.

Rather than spend money on the placebo effect of aphrodisiacs better results are likely to be achieved by relaxing with your partner in a warm bath or shower, or, by soft music and candlelight. This can easily be arranged at home, but if you can go to a restaurant with the right ambiance you may find it acts as a powerful aphrodisiac.

The value of aphrodisiacs in modern medicine is doubtful now that modern drugs, which have been fully tested, are available to stimulate sexual arousal in various different ways. At the same time the existence of these modern sexual stimulants demonstrates that the idea of an aphrodisiac is not beyond the realms of possibility as has sometimes been said by doctors in the past.

Listed below are some of the better known substances which have traditionally been used as aphrodisiacs. None can be recommended without reservation and some are extremely dangerous and should be avoided at all cost. They are listed here so that readers who are so inclined may experiment cautiously with some of them if they feel they may be helpful. If you have an interest in using herbs it is worthwhile consulting a qualified herbalist. Other dangerous or useless concoctions and brews are listed so they may be avoided.

aphrodisiacs that might be worth trying

◆ **Caution**: *Herbal preparations have been used for hundreds and probably thousands of years, but experience of herbs has not been as systematically recorded as has experience of drugs in the modern age and so knowledge of side effects is limited. It must also be remembered that most herbs have not been tested scientifically for side effects in the same way as modern drugs.*

The fact that herbs are "natural" in the sense that they are part of nature provides no guarantee that they do not have harmful effects. It is not natural for people to consume plants except as food, and medicinal herbs are not food. Bear these considerations in mind, be cautious and consult a qualified herbalist if you decide to experiment with some of these substances that claim aphrodisiac properties.

If you take a herbal preparation and have reason to consult your doctor you should tell him or her what you have been taking. It is possible that some of these herbal preparations may interact with drugs that are being taken to assist erection or for any other purpose.

Therefore it is advisable not to experiment with them while taking other drugs but to consider using these aphrodisiacs, if at all, with exercises and modification of diet.

Almond and turnip

Almond *(Prunus amygdalus)* and turnip *(Brassica rapa)* are reputed to be aphrodisiacs in Arab medicine, and are being investigated at King Saud University. The attribution of aphrodisiac properties to almonds may possibly have something to do with the shape of the fruit. The word nut is used for testicles in some languages and the shape of the almond resembles that of a testicle which may do something to encourage belief in its efficacy. Almonds and turnip may be eaten plentifully without any risk to health. Rats fed on turnips or almonds at King Saud University were found to flourish.

Ambergris

Ambergris is a waxy substance taken from the bowel of the sperm whale. Traditionally it has been valued as a sexual stimulant. Recent work at King Saud University, has found that ambrein, an extract of ambergris, increases the sexual activity of male rats. The experiments found that ambrein increases the interest of males in investigating the genital area of females, increases the number of their erections, and the number of times females were successfully mounted by males.

Bee pollen, Royal Jelly

These products made by bees are included in a number of herbal compounds that claim tonic or aphrodisiac properties. They certainly contain some vitamins and may contain other active substances. Not likely to be harmful in any way.

Capsicum

Chilli peppers (capsicums) and cayenne pepper are particularly good sources of a pungent substance called capsaicin. The best known traditional use of capsicum, or capsaicin, in medicine is as a carminative, that is for release of gas from the stomach. However it is also used as a skin irritant and as a pain-relieving rub for use on inflamed joints and lumbago. Creams advertised to enlarge the penis may contain very small quantities of capsicum. The local irritant action of these creams may assist stimulation of the penis. However intercourse immediately after using such a cream would be unwise (unless a condom is used) as the cream may cause vaginal irritation. It would also be extremely unwise and dangerous to try any experimental application of chilli powder to the skin.

Dang gui (Dong Quai)

Chinese herbal authorities say that Dang gui "nourishes the blood" and consider it is the most important tonic herb after ginseng. Dang gui *(Angelica polymorpha var. sinensis)* is used for treatment of anaemia, menstrual problems and after childbirth. It is also a painkiller and laxative and is valued as a tonic for older people, especially women. However it is also used in herbal compounds made for men. The European or Garden Angelica *(Angelica archangelica)* has a reputation as a stimulant of the circulation and is said to warm the hands and feet. It is possible that Dang gui works in a similar way stimulating blood circulation to the extremities including the penis. If so, that might explain why Dang gui is valued as a tonic in old age and sometimes included in formulations that claim an aphrodisiac effect.

Damiana

Damiana *(Turnera diffusa)* is a bitter aromatic herb which grows in Texas and Mexico. It has a purgative action and increases the flow of urine. It is also reputed to have a direct stimulating effect on the male organs. Damiana is recognised as an aphrodisiac by authoritative herbalists such as Mrs M. Grieve *(A Modern Herbal)*. *Potter's New Cyclopaedia* says: "Damiana is very largely prescribed on account of its aphrodisiac qualities, and there is no doubt that it has a very great general and beneficial action on the reproductive organs. It also acts as a tonic to the nervous system". Damiana is readily available through health food stores.

Fenugreek

Fenugreek gives the familiar taste to many Indian curry dishes. Strong curries have developed a reputation for having powerful effects on the body and this herb may account for these. Fenugreek *(Trigonella foenum-graecum)* is said to aid the digestion and have anti-inflammatory properties. Chinese herbalists consider it increases reproductive energy and prescribe the seeds for loss of libido and impotence.

Ginger

Ginger *(Zingiber officinale)* has a reputation as an

aphrodisiac in Arab medicine and is currently being investigated at King Saud University. It does not have a reputation as an aphrodisiac among Western herbalists and it is possible that its reputation in the East simply reflects its "hot" nature. Ginger is readily obtained in food shops and in prepared forms such as tablets from health food stores.

Ginkgo biloba

The leaves of this distinctive tree are said to be helpful when impotence is due to arterial insufficiency *(Journal of Urology, 1989, 141:188A)*. Ginkgo has the reputation backed up by some scientific evidence of improving the circulation of blood in the brain of elderly people. It appears to do this because it contains a substance that activates platelets which play a crucial role in the clotting of blood. Ginkgo can certainly be recommended as a tonic worth trying for the older man, but claims that have sometimes been made for it as an anti-ageing remedy should not be taken seriously.

Ginseng

Panax ginseng, a traditional aphrodisiac, has been shown in experiments at SIU University in the United States and Changsha Medical University in China to stimulate the production of nitrite in the penis, a process which is necessary before the penis can relax and fill with blood. This suggests that there is a physiological basis for the reputation of this herb as an aphrodisiac. It is readily obtained in health food shops.

Gotu kola (Fo Ti, Brahmi)

Gotu kola *(Centella asiatica)* is considered in Indian

Ayurvedic medicine to be the most valuable rejuvenating remedy. Valued for its diuretic (urine stimulating) effect, this herb is said to improve the deficiencies of old age and improve memory. In the West it is traditionally valued for its stimulating, energy-giving effects. It has been used in the East for treatment of skin diseases, including leprosy and sexually transmitted diseases. It has also been used to treat rheumatism and malaria. Mrs M. Grieve warns against large doses in her classic herbal and says that they cause stupor, headache and, in extreme cases, vertigo and coma. Only use in doses recommended by herbal authorities.

Kava kava

Kava kava *(Piper methysticum)* is a pungent root smelling slightly of lilac. It comes originally from the Pacific islands where Polynesian people make it into a fermented drink which is used in their ceremonies for its calming effect and for its ability to expand awareness. Kava kava is a stimulating tonic and diuretic sometimes prescribed by herbalists for genital problems. Before the days of modern drugs it used to be prescribed for the treatment of gonorrhea. It is also reputed to restore vigour to the genital organs in middle age. Herbal authorities warn against using it in pregnancy.

Kola nut (Bissy nut)

Kola nut *(Kola vera)* has a similar effect to coffee, acting as a stimulant to the nervous system. It may be included in patent remedies which claim tonic or aphrodisiac properties. Herbalists describe it as a good general tonic but do not expect any greater effect than you will get from a good cup of coffee.

Muira-puama

Muira-puama is the root of a Brazilian plant *Liriosma ovata*. *Potter's New Cyclopaedia* says: "It is reputed in Brazil to be one of the most powerful aphrodisiacs." It is readily obtained in health food shops.

Oriental herbs

An extract of the root of the plant *Salvia haematodes*, a member of the Sage family, has been found by research at King Saud University to induce sexual behaviour in male rats.

Oyster extract

Oysters have a reputation for having an aphrodisiac effect. The naked appearance of the oyster with its similarity to the mucus parts of the genital organs probably accounts for this idea. Thus the power of the oyster probably depends on sympathetic magic rather than physiology. Some commercial aphrodisiacs contain oyster extract but it is not wise to expect a great deal from such concoctions. On the other hand a plate of oysters in a good restaurant might well assist the relaxation response that leads on to cheerful tumescence.

Prunus africanum and Pygaeum africanum (Red stinkwood)

The bark of these trees is said to enhance the ability to achieve an erection *(Arch. Ital. Urol. Nefrol. Androl, 1991; 63:341-345)* and is also used to treat prostate problems (benign prostatic hyperplasia).

Saw Palmetto

Saw Palmetto is obtained as a green oil extracted from the

berries of the Saw Palmetto (*Serenoa serrulata*). The oil contains steroidal saponins which have a reputation of being effective in the treatment of certain reproductive disorders, particularly prostate problems. Traditionally Saw Palmetto has been used for atrophy of the testes, low male libido and impotence. Available in health food shops or by mail order. It is also used for some female reproductive problems including painful periods and infertility. It is said to stimulate the appetite and build strength.

Tonic foods (amino acids, vitamins etc)

Some mixtures of amino acids, vitamins and other "tonic" substances are advertised for improvement of the libido. It is safe to say that scarcely anyone in the developed world has a shortage of amino acids in their diet. Even the strictest vegetarians obtain plenty of amino acids and so amino acid tonic supplements cannot be recommended. However vitamin deficiencies are more common and might conceivably contribute to a problem with the libido. Older people, heavy smokers, athletes and people with unusual diets may sometimes be deficient in vitamins if they are not eating a well balanced mixed diet containing plenty of fresh foods. A mixed vitamin preparation, obtainable from any chemists, is a more sensible way of correcting a possible deficiency of this kind than a vitamin tonic promoted as an aphrodisiac.

Ylang Ylang

Ylang Ylang oil comes from a perfume tree, *Cananga odorata*, grown in the East Indies. It is said to have anti-depressant and sedative properties and used by aromatherapists for treatment of impotence.

Yohimbine

Yohimbine is derived from the bark of the African tree, *Pausinystalia yohimbe*. It is still sometimes prescribed by doctors for its reputed effect as a sexual tonic or aphrodisiac but is not licensed as a prescription drug in the UK. Yohimbine acts by blocking the activity of certain (alpha-adrenergic) nerves. Some medical evidence suggests that it may work to improve male sexual activity but it has never been tested properly.

Professor Alan Riley of St George's Hospital, London, writes: "Yohimbine. . . has been evaluated in the management of erectile disorder by means of placebo-controlled, but often poorly designed, trials. It does appear to have a modest therapeutic benefit over placebo, particularly in essentially psychogenic erectile disorder, and is generally well tolerated."

Yohimbine is sometimes available as street drug called "yo-yo" and may then be taken in an excessive and dangerous dose. Yohimbine may then cause mental disturbance accompanied by weakness, incoordination, anxiety, headache, nausea, palpitations, and chest pain, sweating, raised blood pressure, fast pulse and breathing. Obtain supplies from a reputable herbalist.

These substances may be dangerous and should not be taken:

Amyl nitrite

Nitrite "poppers" – crushable glass capsules which are broken to release the amyl nitrite – are readily available and used as sexual stimulants. Amyl nitrite causes rapid dilation of veins in the head and neck when it is inhaled. It is used as a treatment for angina (heart pain) bringing rapid relief. It can cause dizziness, headache, vomiting, fainting, low blood pressure and slow pulse, difficulty in breathing and mental disturbance. Nitrite is known to cause relaxation of the cavities in the penis enabling them to fill with blood. It is possible that amyl nitrite has a direct effect of this kind. Amyl nitrate is also used by homosexual men because it assists relaxation of the anal sphincter (the muscle in the anus). But it may also be used because the dramatic and possibly disorienting effects of amyl nitrite on the body become incorporated into sexual rituals. Not recommended.

Cannabis

Cannabis has a reputation as an aphrodisiac and is recommended in some old medical textbooks. It probably works indirectly by inducing relaxation which is a very important preliminary to sexual arousal. However cannabis is an illegal substance and so cannot be recommended. The way in which cannabis will interact with medically recommended drugs is not known.

Cantharides (Spanish Fly)

Of all drugs reputed to have aphrodisiac properties Spanish

Fly is possibly the best known and the most dangerous. Spanish Fly is a greyish brown powder containing shiny green particles and is made by grinding up the dried bodies of a beetle known as *Cantharis vesicatoria*. The active ingredient, which can be obtained in a pure form, is called cantharidin. Cantharidin is a severe irritant to skin and membranes. When taken by mouth it causes irritation to the bowel, lungs, kidney, the bladder and the urethra (urinary tube). This local irritation may cause an erection, and it is this property that has given it its reputation as an aphrodisiac. Cantharides was used in medicine in the 19th century as a blistering agent and counter-irritant but has no use in medicine today. It has extremely dangerous side effects and can cause death when a large dose is taken. It should not be experimented with.

Sometimes Spanish Fly is administered to a person without them knowing it in the vain hope of inducing sexual arousal. This is an extremely foolish thing to do because of the danger from even small doses of Spanish Fly. Symptoms of poisoning from Spanish fly include blood in the urine and/or the faeces, bloody vomit and diffuse injury to the stomach and bowel.

Homeopathic preparations of Spanish Fly are sold by mail order companies. These preparations may be so dilute that they contain none of the original substance. The efficacy of homeopathic preparations has been disputed in medicine for many years. They are generally considered to work, if at all, as a placebo. They cannot be recommended when other efficacious remedies exist.

Catuaba

Catuaba is the name of an aphrodisiac used in Brazil where there is a saying: "until a father reaches 60 the son is his, after that the son is Catuaba's". Catuaba does not seem to be the name of any one plant but rather a name for a number of plants that are believed to have aphrodisiac properties. Due to the uncertainty about the nature of this substance it cannot be recommended.

Gland extracts

Powdered prostate gland, adrenal gland, testicle, and other animal parts such as spinal cord are used in some commercial preparations which claim to benefit older men. Testicle may be described in such preparations as "raw orchic concentrate". These preparations, made by drying and grinding up animal organs, may contain small amounts of hormone that have some effect but the basis for their use is magical rather than rational. There is also a very small risk that spinal cord contains slow viruses of the "mad cow" type. These preparations are probably harmless but cannot be recommended, especially not for vegetarians.

Nettles

Flogging the buttocks with nettles is recommended in some old French medical textbooks as an aphrodisiac. This is an example of a fetishistic practice which might appeal to some men who have special requirements for sexual excitement. A minority of men and women find that practices which involve dominance, submission and other kinds of role-playing are helpful in inducing excitement, but they are a distinct turn-off for others.

Rhinoceros horn and tiger penis.

Animal horns are often seen to be symbols of the male sexual organ, and so by the logic of sympathetic magic a powder made from ground up animal horn or penis is a potent aphrodisiac. Rhino horn, perhaps because of its rarity and expense, is taken to be particularly potent. This is tragic for the rhino which is a severely threatened species, only a few thousand remain in several scattered places round the world.

Toad venom

Chan Su is made from the venom of Chinese toads. The preparation is applied locally to the male genitals. It is extremely dangerous and a number of deaths have occurred among men in New York who have used the drug. Death is caused by induction of an irregular heart rhythm. A West Indian aphrodisiac called Love Stone is also made from toad venom and is equally dangerous.

organisations that provide help

The Impotence Association is an independent organisation which aims to help men who have a problem with potency, and their partners. It is financed by income from patients, doctors and the drug industry. Helpline: 0181 767 7791.

Medical Advisory Service – Impotence Matters Helpline, Tel: 0181 742 7042. Aims to help all men with potency problems

Family Planning Association, 27-29 Mortimer Street, London W1N 7RJ. Tel: 0171 636 7866. Provides information, advice and help on sexual matters as well as contraception. Books on sex available by mail order.

British Association of Counsellors (BAC), 1 Regent Place, Rugby CD21 2PJ. Tel: 0178857 8328. BAC provide a list of counsellors in your area and a list of publications. Send s.a.e.

Brook Centres, 153a East Street, London SE17 2SD. Tel: 0171 708 1234/1390. Provide personal advice and counselling from centres all over the country.

RELATE Marriage Guidance, Herbert Gray College, Little Church Street, Rugby CV21 3AP. Tel: 01788 573241. Relate has psychosexual therapy clinics in a number of centres around the country. The head office can provide details of a centre near you. The organisation is non-profit making and clients are asked to make a contribution towards the cost at each interview. In cases of hardship it may be waived.

Marriage Counselling, Scotland, 105 Hanover Street, Edinburgh EH2 1DJ. Tel: 0131 225 5006. Works in a similar way to RELATE – see above.

The Association of Sexual and Marital Therapists, PO Box 62, Sheffield, S10 3TS. The Association provides a list of counsellors, therapists and clinics in your area. Many work privately. Send a stamped addressed envelope.

Gay Switchboard has contact numbers for counselling and specialist services in most large cities. Get the local number from directory enquiries.

Organisations providing help with illness and disability

British Diabetic Association, 10 Queen Anne Street, London W1M OBD, Tel: 0171 323 1531. The BDA helps diabetics with advice about diets, drugs and insulin, and general guidance on special problems associated with diabetes including impotence.

British Heart Foundation, 14 Fitzhardinge Street, London W1H 4DH. Telephone 0171 935 0185. BHF is a charity supporting research on heart disease, but it also provides information about heart disease including healthy diets and risks of smoking.

Sexual and Personal Relationships for Disabled People (SPOD)
286 Camden Road, London N7 0BJ. Tel: 0171 607 8851. SPOD provides information on sexual matters, organises training and has counsellors all over the UK. It provides telephone counselling and leaflets on physical handicap and sex – positions, methods, devices, and relationships. They also provide special advice for people about sex and multiple sclerosis, sex and arthritis, sex after a heart attack.

DISCERN, 94 Mansfield Road, Nottingham NG1 3HD. Tel: 01602 588043. DISCERN provides advice, counselling and help on all aspects of disability.

Self-Help Direct and its authors

Self-Help Direct Publishing was created by two journalists, Oliver Gillie and Michael Crozier, in 1995 to bring important and useful information direct to the public. It aims to provide people with vital facts about health and other matters, so that they may make crucial decisions for themselves.

We aim to report on the latest medical advances, drugs and treatments for a variety of conditions which may be hard for those not in the medical profession to learn about.

• •

♦ **Oliver Gillie** is a leading medical journalist and author. He was medical correspondent of *The Sunday Times* for 15 years and medical editor of *The Independent* for four years. He has a BSc and a PhD degree from Edinburgh University and worked for several years at the National Institute for Medical Research at Mill Hill, London.

♦ **Susan Aldridge** has a PhD in chemistry and an MSc in biotechnology. Before taking up journalism, she worked for several years as a chemist for the Medical Research Council. Since 1988, she has worked as a freelance journalist and author. She has written three books on genetics and biochemistry. She is medical editor of the monthly science and technology magazine *Focus*.

♦ **Lee Rodwell** is health editor of the popular weekly magazine *Take A Break*. Before becoming a full-time freelance health writer, she was a staff journalist on several national newspapers. She has written many books in health and lifestyle issues and her articles have appeared in magazines and newspapers around the world.

• •

Other books available from Self-Help Direct

Escape from Pain
♦ New ways to fight back with electronic treatment, age-old remedies rediscovered, psycho-strategy, exercises for mind and body. Conventional and alternative – *Escape From Pain* by Oliver Gillie has something for everyone with pain.

Hair Loss: The Answers
♦ In this book, Dr Susan Aldridge aims to explode a few myths and offer real advice and help for men and women concerned about the loss of hair.

You and Your Prostate
♦ The World Health Organisation estimate that 80 per cent of men will eventually need treatment for prostate problems and of these, one in three will need an operation. *You and Your Prostate* by Lee Rodwell offers a full guide to the signs, symptoms and treatment of prostate problems.

♦ *Our promise: If you are not satisfied with any of our books, we will refund your money if you return the book in good condition within 10 days*

Name...

Address...

....

....

....POSTCODE............................

Please send me ....copy/copies of:
❑ **Regaining Potency** @ £10.95
❑ **Escape from Pain** @ £10.95
❑ **Hair Loss: The Answers** @ £10.95
❑ **You and Your Prostate** @ £10.95
❑ I enclose a cheque/postal order made payable to Self-Help Direct, postage and packing included. Overseas sales: $25 per book, including p&p. *Please allow 21 days for delivery.*

ORDERS TO: **SELF-HELP DIRECT, PO BOX 9035, LONDON, N12 8ED**